To my nephews Greyson and Lucas,
for giving me the idea for this book,
and my girls, Zelda, Annabel, and Iggy,
who I hope will use the power of their voices
—J. C.

To my parents, Helen and Victor,
for their endless support of my creative soul
—V. S.

ATHENEUM BOOKS FOR YOUNG READERS • An imprint of Simon & Schuster Children's Publishing Division

1230 Avenue of the Americas, New York, New York 10020

Book design by Greg Stadnyk

Simon & Schuster: Celebrating 100 Years of Publishing in 2024

For information about special discounts for bulk purchases, please contact Simon & Schuster Special Sales at 1-866-506-1949 or business@simonandschuster.com. • The Simon & Schuster Speakers Bureau can bring authors to your live event. For more information or to book an event, contact the Simon & Schuster Speakers Bureau at 1-866-248-3049 or visit our website at www.simonspeakers.com. • The text for this book was set in Excelsior LT Std.

The illustrations for this book were rendered digitally.

Manufactured in China

0424 SCP

First Edition

2 4 6 8 10 9 7 5 3 1

CIP data for this book is available from the Library of Congress.

ISBN 9781665922265

ISBN 9781665922272 (ebook)

SPEAKING OF *America*

UNITED STATES PRESIDENTS AND THE WORDS THAT CHANGED HISTORY

Jared Cohen

Illustrated by Vivian Shih

atheneum

Atheneum Books for Young Readers

NEW YORK LONDON TORONTO SYDNEY NEW DELHI

CONTENTS

Introduction & Guide to This Book

1—George Washington
September 1796 3

2—John Adams
January 1788 5

3—Thomas Jefferson
July 1776 7

4—James Madison
February 1788 9

5—James Monroe
December 1823 11

6—John Quincy Adams
May 1836 13

7—Andrew Jackson
December 1830 15

8—Martin Van Buren
March 1837 17

9—William Henry Harrison
March 1841 19

10—John Tyler
April 1841 21

11—James K. Polk
May 1846 23

12—Zachary Taylor
July 1850 25

13—Millard Fillmore
October 1850 27

14—Franklin Pierce
December 1855 29

15—James Buchanan
January 1861 31

16—Abraham Lincoln
November 1863 33

17—Andrew Johnson
February 1868 35

18—Ulysses S. Grant
April 1865 37

19—Rutherford B. Hayes
December 1880 39

20—James A. Garfield
March 1881 41

21—Chester A. Arthur
December 1881 43

22 & 24—Grover Cleveland
December 1887 45

23—Benjamin Harrison
February 1893 47

25—William McKinley
March 1897 .... *49*

26—Theodore Roosevelt
April 1910 .... *51*

27—William Howard Taft
October 1911 .... *53*

28—Woodrow Wilson
April 1917 .... *55*

29—Warren G. Harding
May 1920 .... *57*

30—Calvin Coolidge
July 1926 .... *59*

31—Herbert Hoover
August 1928 .... *61*

32—Franklin D. Roosevelt
March 1933 .... *63*

33—Harry S. Truman
March 1947 .... *65*

34—Dwight D. Eisenhower
January 1961 .... *67*

35—John F. Kennedy
September 1962 .... *69*

36—Lyndon B. Johnson
March 1965 .... *71*

37—Richard Nixon
August 1974 .... *73*

38—Gerald R. Ford
August 1974 .... *75*

39—Jimmy Carter
July 1979 .... *77*

40—Ronald Reagan
June 1987 .... *79*

41—George H. W. Bush
January 1991 .... *81*

42—Bill Clinton
January 1993 .... *83*

43—George W. Bush
September 2001 .... *85*

44—Barack Obama
January 2008 .... *87*

45—Donald Trump
June 2015 .... *89*

46—Joe Biden
January 2021 .... *91*

Presidential Time Line

Delivering Your Message

What If?

Introduction & Guide to This Book

My fellow Americans!

Today, we recognize these words immediately. This is how the president of the United States often starts important speeches and announcements. It's a phrase the presidents use to make their audience feel like a part of something *big*—to feel like being an American unites them with the millions of other people who live across fifty different states, the District of Columbia, and the five major US territories. Most of these people will never meet each other. But they share one country. They are fellow Americans.

But even though this phrase is recognizable to Americans today, it wasn't always. "My fellow Americans" got its start in presidential speechmaking in the last century. Franklin Delano Roosevelt, America's thirty-second president, was the first to regularly say "my fellow Americans" in his big speeches—more than 150 years after the country was founded! This phrase is just one example, among many, of how what the presidents say—and why and how they say it—has been evolving since George Washington's time.

This is a book about what America's presidents have said and how their words have shaped history—from policies and ideas to the changing way Americans think about themselves and their country's place in the world. Some of the words in this book are famous, like the ones Thomas Jefferson used to open the Declaration of Independence: *"We hold these truths to be self-evident. . . ."* And some of them—both the speeches and perhaps even the speakers—are relatively unknown. When was the last time you came across a quotable line from Franklin Pierce? The answer is: you're about to!

Reading what the presidents said, in their own words, can be challenging. People spoke differently in 1776, 1863, and even 1941 than they do today. Sometimes presidential speeches can sound stuffy and be difficult to understand. But the words of America's presidents have changed the course of history—both in the United States and all around the world. There's no better way to understand history than to go straight to the source, hearing directly from the people who made it.

As of this writing, there have been forty-five presidents of the United States (some people count Grover Cleveland twice because he served two nonconsecutive terms, but we won't do that here). This book includes remarks from every one of them. The subjects of these quotes include everything from war and peace to civil rights, from the moon landing to Ground Zero in New York City after 9/11. America's presidents have had something to say about almost every moment in United States history, even before there *was* a United States.

Each president's quote is unpacked in four sections:

The World in the Year of the Quote: A look at what was happening in America (and around the world) at the time of the president's remarks.

Words Have a Purpose: What the president meant by the quote, why he chose the words he did, and how he considered his audience when speaking.

Words Make a Difference: The real-world consequences of the quote and its impact on American history.

Did You Know?: Some presidential fun facts and interesting context you may not have been aware of. For example, did you know that one president spoke Dutch as his first language? (Don't worry, though—all the quotes in this book are in English!)

The speeches and written remarks included here are just a snapshot of American history, and I hope that you'll see them as an invitation to learn even more. Keep in mind that there was much more going on at every point than we can get into in just one book, and that there are also multiple ways of interpreting *any* set of remarks or set of events. Though this book covers a lot, it can't cover everything.

Learning about history requires both an open mind and independent thinking. We must remain curious about the past as we reflect for ourselves on what it meant and how it affects us today. I invite you to turn the page and begin with the president who started it all: George Washington.

GEORGE WASHINGTON

"Observe good faith and justice towards all Nations; cultivate peace and harmony with all."

George Washington, Farewell Address, September 17, 1796 (printed September 19, 1796)

The World in 1796

George Washington was America's first president, and the United States was one of the youngest countries in the world. There's nothing normal about founding a new country, and everything America's first president did in office was new. After all, the Declaration of Independence had been signed just twenty years before, in 1776, and the Revolutionary War had ended only thirteen years before, in 1783. What the United States would do with its newfound independence was anyone's guess.

So when Washington left office, it was a big deal. At that point, America had only ever had one president! And in most countries, the transfer of power from one leader to the next was not peaceful. Washington saw this uncertainty and used his farewell address to do more than just say goodbye. He took this opportunity to caution the young country against conflict, both externally and from within.

Words Have a Purpose

When Washington left office, the United States was not as powerful as it is today. France and Great Britain were the strongest countries in the world. And they were at war with each other! Some Americans favored Great Britain, and some favored France. But Washington argued that America should not take sides. He wanted the United States to grow stronger by trading with both France *and* Great Britain, instead of making enemies when it didn't need to. The young country was lucky: Europe was far away, and there was no reason to get involved in fights across the Atlantic unnecessarily.

When Washington spoke, Americans listened. After all, he'd led the new country to independence in the Revolutionary War! The United States stayed out of European wars for years. Washington believed that this policy would help the country get stronger over time, saying that America would one day be "a great Nation."

Words Make a Difference

George Washington's farewell address took many by surprise. It was published in September 1796, just two months before the next presidential election. Many Americans thought Washington would be president for a long time—maybe even for life. The people were used to kings, after all! But Washington was not a monarch. By choosing to announce his retirement, he set a powerful example for the new country, establishing as precedent the peaceful transfer of power that is essential for any democracy.

George Washington established the tradition of a two-term limit on the presidency. Only Franklin D. Roosevelt, who won four consecutive elections, broke this tradition. But in 1951, with the Twenty-Second Amendment to the Constitution, the two-term limit became the law of the land. Washington's example had stuck and was now unbreakable.

> *"Children should be educated and instructed in the principles of freedom."*
>
> John Adams, *A Defence of the Constitutions of Government of the United States of America*, January 1788

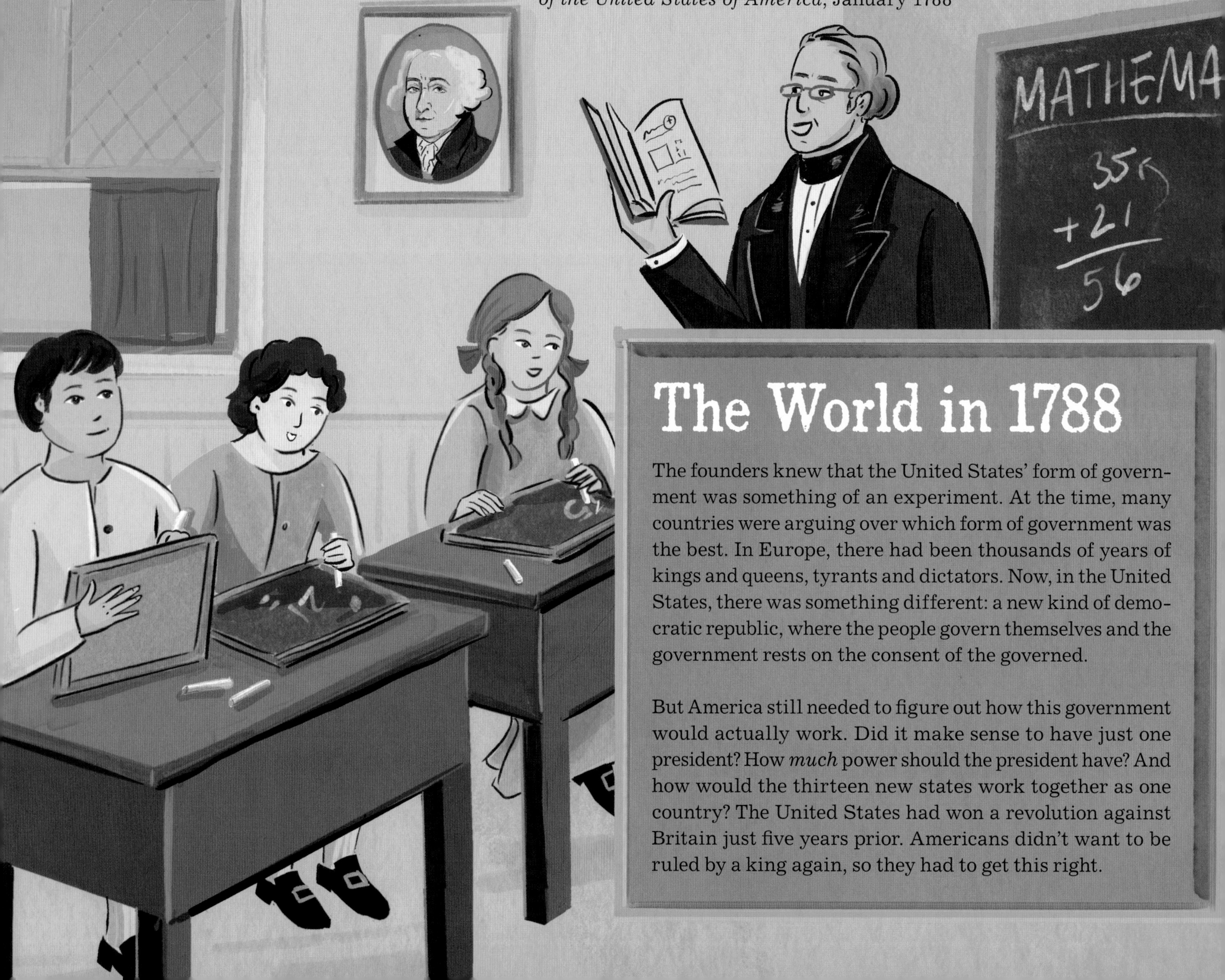

The World in 1788

The founders knew that the United States' form of government was something of an experiment. At the time, many countries were arguing over which form of government was the best. In Europe, there had been thousands of years of kings and queens, tyrants and dictators. Now, in the United States, there was something different: a new kind of democratic republic, where the people govern themselves and the government rests on the consent of the governed.

But America still needed to figure out how this government would actually work. Did it make sense to have just one president? How *much* power should the president have? And how would the thirteen new states work together as one country? The United States had won a revolution against Britain just five years prior. Americans didn't want to be ruled by a king again, so they had to get this right.

Words Have a Purpose

In 1787, delegates debated these questions at the Constitutional Convention in Philadelphia. Adams was in Europe, serving as an American ambassador to Great Britain. But he wanted to be a part of the debate too—so he wrote a three-volume book that explained America's emerging system of government not just to the American people but to the entire world. Among other ideas, Adams wanted to show that separating powers among three branches of government—executive, legislative, and judicial—was a good decision.

Adams knew that for America's experiment in self-government to work, confidence in it had to be passed down through the generations. For this to happen, Adams believed the American people needed to understand their rights and freedoms, which were laid out in the Declaration of Independence and the Constitution. But just as importantly, they also needed to understand that their freedoms came with a *responsibility* to be good citizens. And being good citizens meant being educated about the "principles of freedom" on which the United States was founded.

Words Make a Difference

The Founding Fathers cared about America's children. And not just their own children (although John and Abigail Adams had high hopes for their six kids, especially future president John Quincy Adams). *All* of America's children were important, because the success of the new government depended on them. America's founders could get a lot of things right. But for the new country to survive, every new generation had to be taught why the framework of self-government was important. Adams's words resonate even today, as young people continue to learn what it means to be American.

John Adams was the first president to live in the White House (even though it wasn't called that at the time). When Adams moved into the White House in November 1800, Washington, DC, was still more of a construction zone than a city. He had to move out just a few months later because he lost the next election to his own vice president: Thomas Jefferson.

THOMAS JEFFERSON

"We hold these truths to be self-evident, that all men are created equal, that they are endowed by their Creator with certain unalienable Rights, that among these are Life, Liberty and the pursuit of Happiness."

Thomas Jefferson, Declaration of Independence, July 4, 1776

The World in 1776

We're going back in time to the country's beginning, because these are the words that founded America. In 1776, fifty-six prominent Americans—some of the colonies' most well-known lawyers, doctors, scholars, and statesmen—signed the Declaration of Independence.

The Declaration explained why the thirteen American colonies had chosen to break away from Great Britain, the most powerful empire in the world. It included a long list of reasons for this decision: The colonies were taxed too heavily. They had no representation in the British government. They were subject to harsh laws. And the British could be brutal rulers, as evidenced by deadly events like the Boston Massacre, when British troops shot and killed five Bostonians protesting in a crowd.

Words Make a Difference

Even though Thomas Jefferson and the fifty-five other delegates who signed the Declaration of Independence argued that everyone is created equal and that all people have unalienable rights, not *everyone's* rights were protected. It was a very unequal society. Many of the Founding Fathers enslaved Black people, who were brought to the colonies in chains. Women couldn't vote. Native Americans were often abused and mistreated. There were many manifestations of suffering and inequality.

These were terrible injustices, with legacies that persist to this day. The reality of the United States in 1776 did not reflect the principles in the Declaration of Independence. But countless Americans throughout history have refused to lose sight of these founding principles, which set the United States apart. Abolitionists, civil rights leaders, suffragettes, and many others have worked for decades—even centuries—to deliver on the Declaration of Independence's promise of unalienable rights for *everyone* in America. That work continues today!

Words Have a Purpose

Jefferson's words changed the course of history forever. The first few sentences of the Declaration are probably the most famous ever written by an American in a political document. No country had ever been founded on the principle that citizens have fundamental rights their government was established to protect. This concept set the American Revolution apart. At the time, it was truly revolutionary.

☞ DID YOU KNOW?

The Declaration of Independence has inspired many people throughout history in their own fights for freedom. In 1848, the American women's rights movement issued the Declaration of Sentiments at the Seneca Falls Convention. In 1863, Frederick Douglass and Abraham Lincoln each revisited the Declaration when they called for emancipation. A century later, Dr. Martin Luther King Jr. called the Declaration a "promissory note" in his famous "I Have a Dream" speech, arguing that the Declaration was a guarantee of protection for the rights of every American throughout history, not just those in 1776. And independence movements around the world—from Haiti, to Israel, to Kosovo—have taken inspiration from the Declaration of Independence and its promise of life, liberty, and the pursuit of happiness.

JAMES MADISON

"If men were angels, no government would be necessary."

James Madison, Federalist 51, February 8, 1788

The World in 1788

The Revolutionary War was over, and America had won. Now, the victorious revolutionaries faced the difficult task of making thirteen new states unite as one country. The states needed one government, otherwise they'd each go their different ways. Because the existing laws weren't doing the job, the country's founders needed to draft a constitution: a framework of government and national laws that all citizens agreed on.

So in 1787, delegates from twelve of the thirteen states met in Philadelphia to write the American Constitution. They spent a hot summer debating in Philadelphia's Independence Hall and came up with a draft. Now the last big hurdle was getting each state to hold its own convention and ratify (or approve) the new Constitution. If the states couldn't all agree to uphold what the delegates in Philadelphia had written, America wouldn't *have* a constitution holding it together.

Words Have a Purpose

In a democracy, citizens have to persuade each other if they want to make changes. Madison's words were part of one of the most important arguments in American history: whether or not to ratify the new Constitution. On one side of the debate were the Anti-Federalists, who thought the proposed Constitution would give way too much power to the federal government. And on the other were the Federalists, who thought America needed one strong, central government.

If there was one thing that almost all Americans agreed on, it was that giving too much power to just one person was a bad idea—especially if that person hadn't been chosen by the people. But the United States did need *some* sort of leadership. So the American Constitution proposed something that had never been tried on such a grand scale: a democratic republic that required the people to settle their differences by voting, not fighting. Within the federal government, power would be separated among the legislative branch (Congress), the executive branch (the president), and the judicial branch (the courts). Congress would make the laws, the executive branch would carry out the laws, and the judicial branch would interpret the laws if there were disputes. Within each state, power would be shared between state and local officials to ensure decisions were made by the people most accountable to the voters.

Words Make a Difference

To sway states in favor of the Federalist position, three of the founders—Alexander Hamilton, James Madison, and John Jay—wrote eighty-five anonymous essays. These essays were read far and wide in newspapers across the country. They helped convince all thirteen states, each filled with people who had diverse perspectives, to ratify the Constitution. Today, these essays are known as the Federalist Papers.

The American Constitution has stood the test of time—at more than 230 years old, it's now the oldest democratic governing document in the world! For his work at the Constitutional Convention, James Madison is known as the Father of the Constitution.

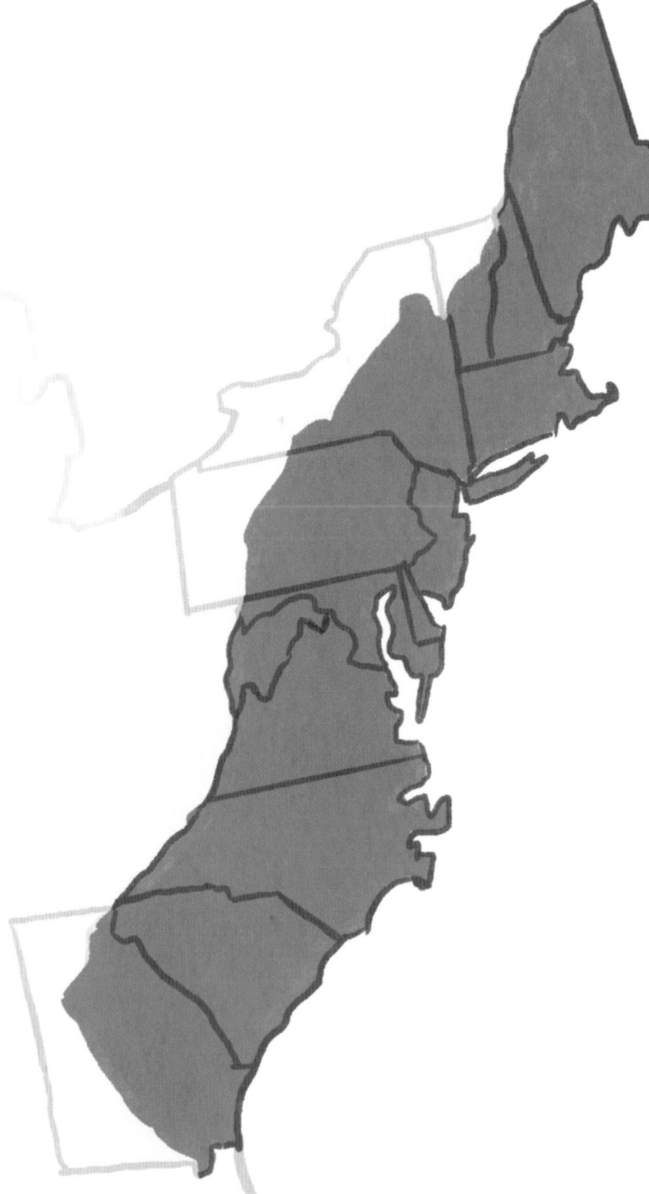

JAMES MONROE

"The American continents, by the free and independent condition which they have assumed and maintain, are henceforth not to be considered as subjects for future colonization by any European powers."

James Monroe, Monroe Doctrine, December 2, 1823

The World in 1823

James Monroe was president during the "Era of Good Feelings." The United States had survived the War of 1812 with the United Kingdom (the new term for the united kingdoms of Great Britain and Ireland). With war in the rearview mirror, many Americans were pretty happy with the direction of the country. President Monroe was very popular—he won almost every vote in the election of 1820. But unfortunately, the "good feelings" were about to go away. The biggest debates of the nineteenth century (slavery and westward expansion) were becoming even more divisive. Most of the Founding Fathers had died, and no one in the new generation of leaders had the stature of George Washington or Thomas Jefferson.

James Monroe was one of the last Founding Fathers, and Americans looked to him for help figuring out the country's place in a changing world. Monroe soon got the chance to set a strong example of what American leadership could look like after many former Spanish colonies in Latin America won their own independence. When European empires tried to regain control of their old colonies, Monroe stood in the way. He issued what would become known as the Monroe Doctrine: a declaration that there would henceforth be no new colonization, or even intervention, by Europe in the Western Hemisphere.

5

☞ DID YOU KNOW?

The Monroe Doctrine was a way for the United States to stand up to European empires in the Western Hemisphere. But at least one European empire *loved* it: the United Kingdom. The UK didn't want its rival Spain to reassert itself in Latin America. The UK government even suggested that it should announce the doctrine with the United States! In the end, though, Monroe made the declaration on his own.

Words Have a Purpose

The Monroe Doctrine was a major announcement of America's emerging role in the world. America was growing more confident, and Monroe made it clear that the country intended to stand up for itself and its neighbors. Many European countries still had stronger navies and armies than the United States, but they were beginning to see their former colonies as more of an equal. The Monroe Doctrine would become a bedrock of American foreign policy for years to come.

Words Make a Difference

American presidents have turned to the Monroe Doctrine throughout the United States' history. In 1865, the US Secretary of State invoked the Monroe Doctrine when supporting the president of Mexico against a French invasion. In 1895, Grover Cleveland used it to help settle an argument between Venezuela and the United Kingdom. In 1904, Theodore Roosevelt gave it a big update with the "Roosevelt Corollary." Finally, in 1962, John F. Kennedy invoked it when the Soviet Union deployed ballistic missiles in nearby Cuba.

"Am I gagged or am I not?"

John Quincy Adams, Address to the House of Representatives, May 25, 1836

The World in 1836

No person has ever been better prepared to become president than John Quincy Adams. But after a lifetime of getting ready for the job, he lost his reelection bid in 1828. But Adams didn't quit! Instead, he was elected to the House of Representatives (one of the two chambers of Congress, along with the Senate). Adams's time in the House coincided with some of America's most significant debates about slavery.

Slavery had divided Northern states and Southern states—as well as abolitionists and enslavers—since the country's founding in 1776. Many people believed the issue was so explosive that it could lead to civil war, and that it was too dangerous for Congress to even mention. Adams strongly disagreed. He believed that the American people wanted their elected representatives to debate slavery, and that it was the duty of Congress to do just that. But the enslavers in Congress tried to keep him quiet, passing a "gag rule" that prevented any mention of slavery in the House.

DID YOU KNOW?

John Quincy Adams was the only former president who later served in the House of Representatives. He was a member of Congress until he suffered a fatal stroke on the House floor in 1848, at age 80. The couch he died on is still in the United States Capitol, in a room just off the Old House Chamber.

Words Have a Purpose

John Quincy Adams's opponents issued the gag rule because they knew how powerful his words were. Many members of Congress didn't want to talk openly about slavery, whether because they wanted slavery to continue or because they thought even debating the issue would tear the country apart. They sought to stifle any debate before it could even begin.

But John Quincy Adams fought back. He knew that the First Amendment guaranteed Americans the right to speak and to send Congress petitions (expressions of their views, or requests for action from the government). Adams was determined to give those Americans a voice. Slowly but surely, the abolitionist cause rallied around Adams as its greatest congressional champion.

Words Make a Difference

John Quincy Adams was one of the newest members of Congress, but he was also a former president. When he spoke, people listened. He kept up the fight against the gag rule for years.

Adams wouldn't let Congress forget that a significant portion of the American people—especially religious groups like the Quakers, many of them led by women—were anti-slavery. He tried to read their petitions every time Congress met, in spite of the gag rule. And over time, John Quincy Adams became an outspoken abolitionist himself.

Sadly, Adams didn't live to see abolition become a reality. But he *did* get a win when Congress got rid of the gag rule and slavery was once more up for debate in the House of Representatives. By the time Adams passed away, a young Illinois congressman named Abraham Lincoln had come to Washington. With Adams gone, Lincoln would continue the fight to abolish slavery.

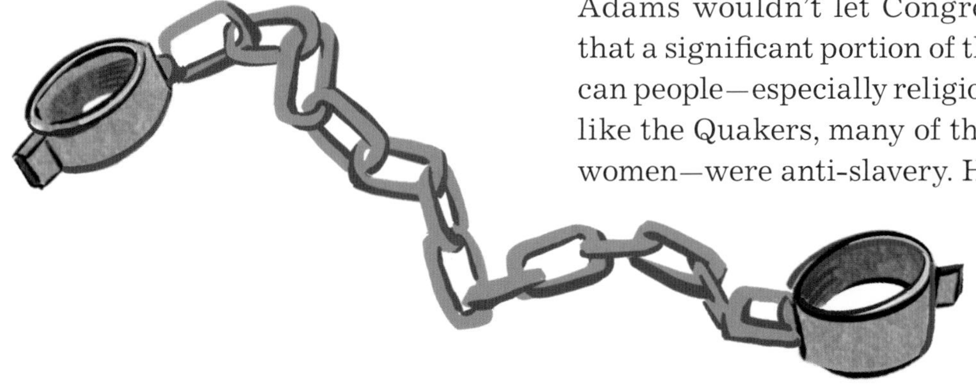

ANDREW JACKSON

"It gives me pleasure to announce to Congress that the benevolent policy of the Government, steadily pursued for nearly thirty years, in relation to the removal of the Indians beyond the white settlements is approaching to a happy consummation."

Andrew Jackson, Message to Congress, December 6, 1830

The World in 1830

Americans descended from Europeans and Africans were by no means the first people to inhabit the land that is now the United States, or the rest of North and South America. For hundreds of years, European colonists had come to the Americas from countries such as the United Kingdom, France, Spain, and the Netherlands, and they'd transported enslaved people from Africa. But for even longer, millions of Native Americans had inhabited the two continents, living in hundreds of communities for *thousands* of years—long before Christopher Columbus crossed the Atlantic Ocean in 1492.

Native Americans were often treated very badly. As the United States population grew, its citizens demanded more land to build new homes, farms, and towns. But that land was often already inhabited by Native Americans. The United States government used a variety of methods to expand its settlements anyway, from purchasing and bargaining to taking land by force.

This expansion came to a head in 1830, when Andrew Jackson convinced Congress to pass the Indian Removal Act. This new law gave Jackson and his administration the power to forcibly send Native Americans to other parts of the country, where they'd never lived before.

7

Words Have a Purpose

Jackson may have been happy to make the announcement. He may have seen his new policies as "benevolent," meaning kind or charitable. But certainly not everyone felt that way. Some Americans objected. And the overwhelming majority of Native American people didn't want to be removed from their ancestral lands, which had been incorporated into the United States as states like Georgia, Alabama, Mississippi, and Tennessee. They'd lived on these lands for generations—long before any Europeans set foot there.

Words Make a Difference

Andrew Jackson moved fast to implement the Indian Removal Act. Tens of thousands of Native Americans were removed from their homes and relocated to places that were mostly unsettled and remote. Thousands of Native Americans died from disease, starvation, and the hardships of the journey. And life was difficult for those who did survive.

When Native American tribes, like the Cherokee Nation, didn't want to trade away their land, the US military pushed them out anyway, forcing them to walk hundreds of miles to new territories. This expulsion was called the "Trail of Tears," because the journey brought sickness, suffering, and death to so many Native American people. The Native communities that survived continue to live in the United States and contribute to the American way of life, and it's important for all Americans to learn about their history and present-day experiences.

DID YOU KNOW?

As a teenager during the Revolutionary War, Andrew Jackson was taken prisoner by the British. When he refused to polish a British officer's boots, the soldier drew his sword and slashed Jackson's face. The future president had a long scar from the wound for the rest of his life.

MARTIN VAN BUREN

"From a small community we have risen to a people powerful in numbers and in strength."

Martin Van Buren, Inaugural Address, March 4, 1837

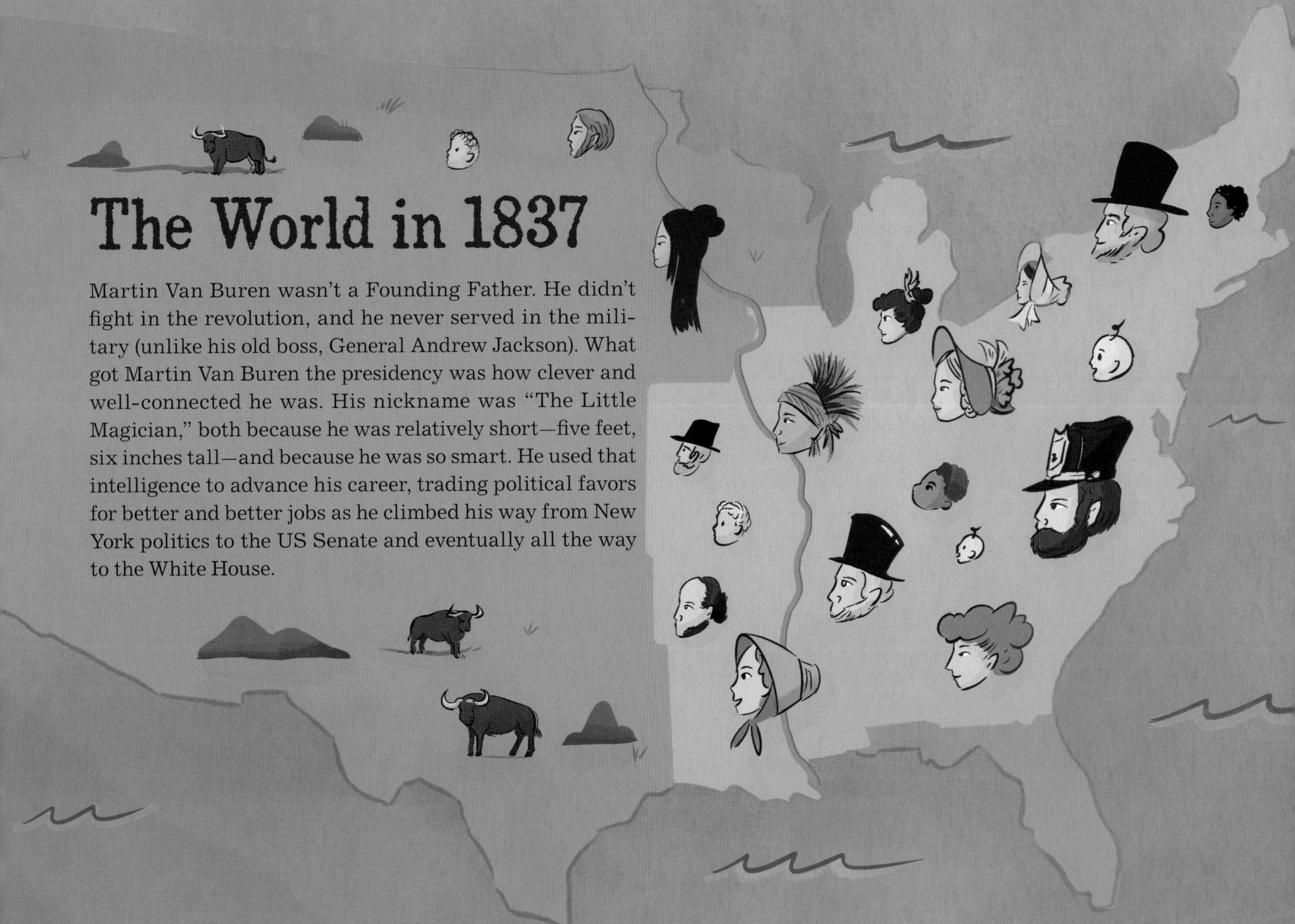

The World in 1837

Martin Van Buren wasn't a Founding Father. He didn't fight in the revolution, and he never served in the military (unlike his old boss, General Andrew Jackson). What got Martin Van Buren the presidency was how clever and well-connected he was. His nickname was "The Little Magician," both because he was relatively short—five feet, six inches tall—and because he was so smart. He used that intelligence to advance his career, trading political favors for better and better jobs as he climbed his way from New York politics to the US Senate and eventually all the way to the White House.

8

Words Have a Purpose

By the time Martin Van Buren took office in 1837, America had changed significantly since its founding. Van Buren's inaugural address was kind of like a report card. He gave the speech just over sixty years after the Declaration of Independence was signed. How was America doing?

In his speech, Van Buren acknowledged the challenges America faced, but he gave a very positive report overall. The American population was growing because of new births and new immigration. More and more Americans were moving west—and as states like Arkansas and Michigan joined the Union, what Americans considered "west" was also changing. The United States was growing more prosperous, and its cities were becoming trading destinations.

But the good times probably weren't going to last forever. With westward expansion, there were more questions about the future, as Congress had to debate whether each new state would allow slavery within its borders or not. Just a few months after Van Buren's address, the Panic of 1837 sent the booming economy into a tailspin that lasted into the 1840s. Van Buren couldn't have known that was going to happen—but if he had, he probably wouldn't have said so in an inaugural address. People usually want to hear good news in the president's first speech!

Words Make a Difference

Martin Van Buren isn't remembered as one of the greatest speakers in American history. But behind closed doors, he was one of the most persuasive politicians of his generation. By this time, political parties (organized groups of Americans with similar political beliefs and interests) were an important fact of American life. Van Buren was a master politician who could mobilize political parties to his advantage. In his home state of New York, he became a "party boss": someone who stays out of the spotlight but still maintains a lot of influence and power, effectively controlling what their political party decides to do. This role didn't give Van Buren much opportunity for fancy speeches. But sometimes, what you say in private can be as important as what you say in public.

Martin Van Buren was the only American president whose first language wasn't English. He grew up in Kinderhook, New York, in a community of people who emigrated from the Netherlands. He spoke Dutch at home.

WILLIAM HENRY HARRISON

"Fellow-citizens, being fully invested with that high office to which the partiality of my countrymen has called me, I now take an affectionate leave of you."

William Henry Harrison, Inaugural Address, March 4, 1841

INAUGURATION OF W.H. HARRISON

The World in 1841

In 1841, William Henry Harrison was the oldest president America had ever had. He was sixty-eight years old on his inauguration day. That may not seem so old these days, because people live much longer now. But at the time, Harrison was older than the United States!

Harrison was also the first American president from the Whig Party, a new group in American politics. The new president from the new party made a huge entrance on Inauguration Day. He got to Washington on a train—the first president to make his arrival with this relatively new technology. Then he rode up the main road on his favorite horse, a white stallion named Whitey. He had a huge crowd (more than fifty thousand people) waiting for him. It was a big day!

But Harrison's first day in office was his best. He didn't last long. He died just thirty-one days later, on April 4, 1841. His was the shortest presidency in American history.

9

Words Have a Purpose

William Henry Harrison was the first person from the Whig Party to become president. The Whigs may not be around anymore, but back then, they were a major force in American politics. Some of the most prominent political figures of the time—not just Harrison, but also Henry Clay from Kentucky and Daniel Webster from Massachusetts—were Whigs. With this new political party in charge, Americans were eager to hear what the president's plans were.

But whatever his plans, Harrison wouldn't have much time to enact them. When he told his audience that he was going to "take an affectionate leave" of them, he was unknowingly foreshadowing his own death.

Words Make a Difference

Though there were fifty thousand people in attendance, few remembered William Henry Harrison's inaugural address. What they *did* remember was how long it was (8,445 words, to be exact). Harrison's speech lasted an hour and forty-five minutes. The audience got bored, wandering off and stamping their feet in the cold to keep warm. Some long speeches are said to "bore the audience to death." In Harrison's unfortunate case, that was almost literally true.

DID YOU KNOW?

Most people think that William Henry Harrison died of pneumonia. Inauguration Day was very cold; he didn't wear a coat or gloves; and his speech was extremely long, so he was outside for a while. It stands to reason that the old man got sick that day—and died because of it.

However, it's since been discovered that Harrison's cause of death likely wasn't pneumonia, but an illness brought on by deadly bacteria in the White House sewer system. Other presidents would later suffer from the same disease.

JOHN TYLER

"I can never consent to being dictated to as to what I shall or shall not do. I, as president, shall be responsible for my administration."

John Tyler, in response to his secretary of state, April 6, 1841

The World in 1841

John Tyler was America's first "accidental president." To date, eight American presidents have died in office. But when William Henry Harrison passed away in 1841, it had never happened before. Vice President Tyler wasn't even in Washington, DC, at the time! He was home in Virginia, and he had to hurry back to town. If Tyler was going to inherit the title, he would have to put up a fight.

Words Have a Purpose

When John Tyler had his first meeting with his cabinet—the group of people who run the president's executive departments, such as the Department of State and Department of the Treasury—they were upset. They'd all been chosen for their roles by William Henry Harrison, and they didn't like the idea of being bossed around by Tyler. So they had an idea: What if, instead of the president making all the decisions, the cabinet voted on them instead? That way, *they* would have power, and Tyler wouldn't.

But of course, Tyler didn't want that. He said that *he* was the president, so *he* was in charge. He wasn't going to be told what to do by a vote of his cabinet—he was going to make his own decisions. The cabinet, and the American people, would have to get used to that.

Words Make a Difference

When American policymakers don't know what to do, they turn to the Constitution. It's a kind of instruction manual for the American government. No president had ever died in office before Harrison, so Americans looked to the text of the Constitution for answers about what to do next.

They didn't get a lot of clarity. The section of the Constitution about what happens when a president dies is a mouthful: *"In Case of the Removal of the President from Office, or of his Death, Resignation, or Inability to discharge the Powers and Duties of the said Office, the Same shall devolve on the Vice President."*

These words were confusing, to say the least. What does "the same" mean? And how does an office "devolve" on anyone? John Tyler said he knew the answer: he was now the president! But not everyone agreed. Tyler's kinder critics said he should be called "the acting president." The meaner ones said he should be called "His Accidency," since it was only by accident that he had the job at all.

Still, Tyler held firm, and his precedent stuck. Any time a US president has died in office since, the vice president has assumed the presidency, just like John Tyler.

☞ DID YOU KNOW?

On February 28, 1844, Tyler almost died, too! He was on a ship when a cannon exploded and killed several people, including his secretary of state and secretary of the navy. The incident claimed more lives of top government officials than any other event in American history. And it nearly made America's first accidental president the second president ever to die in office.

JAMES K. POLK

"As war exists, and, notwithstanding all our efforts to avoid it, exists by the act of Mexico herself, we are called upon by every consideration of duty and patriotism to vindicate with decision the honor, the rights, and the interests of our country."

James K. Polk, Special Message to Congress on Mexican Relations, May 11, 1846

The World in 1846

In 1846, the biggest issue facing the United States was Texas. The territory had effectively won independence from Mexico ten years prior, becoming its own country until it was annexed by the United States in December 1845. This was a late Christmas present for James K. Polk, for whom westward expansion was always top of mind.

Polk was a big believer in a concept called Manifest Destiny—the belief that it was the United States' fate to span the entire North American continent—and he was making it a reality. By 1846, the UK had signed a treaty granting the United States the territory of Oregon and marking a new northern US border on the forty-ninth parallel. But Mexico controlled the future territories of California and New Mexico, and it hadn't given up hope of regaining Texas.

War was coming. Polk sent General Zachary Taylor to the edge of Texas with several thousand troops, seeking a stronger negotiating position with Mexico. But when negotiations failed and Taylor's troops got close, the Mexican forces attacked, and the Mexican-American War was on.

Words Have a Purpose

The president was asking Congress to make a declaration of war against Mexico. But Taylor's troops and the Mexican army were shooting at each other over the Rio Grande already. Everyone understood that this could lead to a larger war, but Polk wanted Congress to make an explicit declaration so he could justify more military action against Mexico.

Polk had created a perfect situation to get Congress on his side, because he could now honestly say that Mexico had shot first. That was enough for the Senate, which voted to declare war two days after Polk's speech. The president had his war—and with more than fifty thousand men under his command, it looked like he would win.

Words Make a Difference

Two years later, the United States won the Mexican-American War. The peace treaty signed in February 1848 granted the United States the territories of what are now California, Nevada, Utah, New Mexico, Texas, and most of Arizona and Colorado. This was a *huge* deal. Mexico lost half of its land in exchange for little more than $15 million. But even if Polk was pleased to gain so much territory, victory came at a cost. Every time new territories were added to the Union, the issue of slavery came up. Would these new lands become slave states, or free? Who would get to decide? Heated debates over these questions would bring the country closer and closer to civil war.

Some of the generals who later became famous in the Civil War got their start in the Mexican-American War. Confederates like Robert E. Lee and Stonewall Jackson, as well as Union leaders like Ulysses S. Grant and Winfield Scott Hancock, all fought together then—but a few years later, many of them would fight for opposing sides.

ZACHARY TAYLOR

"I have always done my duty. I am ready to die. My only regret is for the friends I leave behind me."

Zachary Taylor, on the day of his death, July 9, 1850

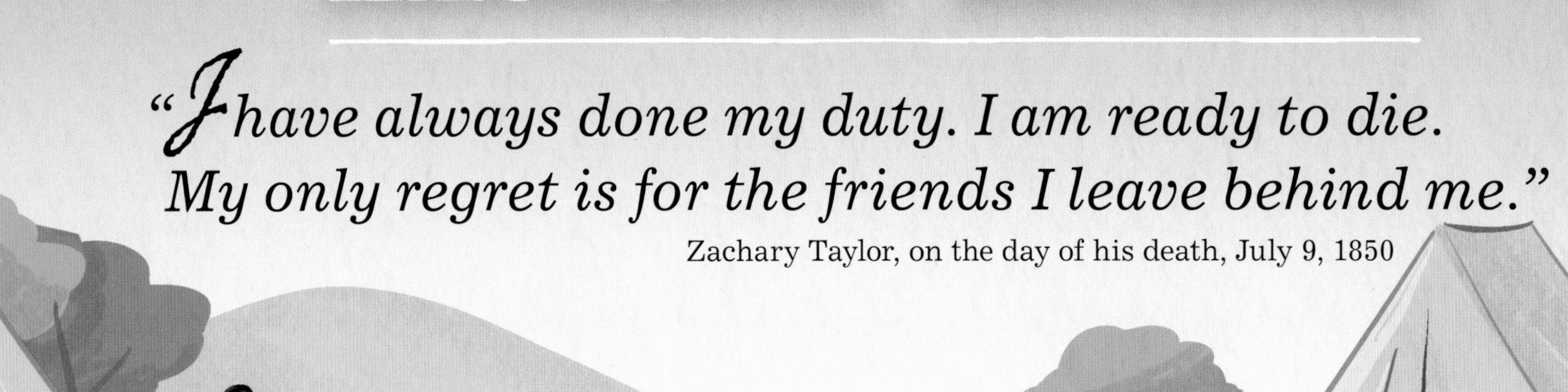

The World in 1850

Zachary Taylor was the most popular man in America. As a general during the Mexican-American War, he won victories on the battlefield and in the hearts and minds of the men under his command. His nickname was "Old Rough and Ready," because everyone knew that Zachary Taylor would do the hard work, roll up his sleeves, and get his hands dirty, right alongside his soldiers. He rode that popularity straight to the White House.

After the Mexican-American War, the United States had lots of new territory on its hands, including modern-day Texas, California, Nevada, and Utah, as well as chunks of other states, like Colorado, Oklahoma, Kansas, and Wyoming. This new territory meant plenty of hard work ahead for the Taylor White House, which had to accommodate free and slave states alike.

12

The number one danger for presidents in the nineteenth century wasn't assassination—the top presidential killer was contaminated White House drinking water. Dirty water may have killed Zachary Taylor, James K. Polk, and William Henry Harrison.

Words Have a Purpose

Zachary Taylor had survived the battlefield, but he wouldn't survive the White House. He died in office on July 9, 1850, only sixteen months after becoming president. What killed him was a terrible stomach virus—which he may have gotten from eating raw, unwashed produce or drinking infected water from the White House tap on a hot summer day. Always a soldier, Taylor wanted his family and friends to know that he'd been thinking about his job as president to the end.

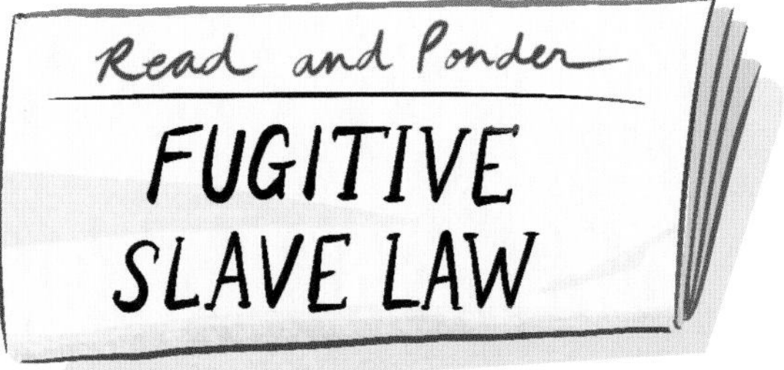

Words Make a Difference

Members of the military often have a sense of duty or obligation to their country. In America, they take oaths to support and defend the Constitution of the United States. And veterans who become presidents usually bring that sense of duty and patriotism to the White House.

Zachary Taylor may have thought he'd done his duty, and he may not have had any regrets about his leadership. But much of his legacy was about to be tossed aside by his successor. His vice president, Millard Fillmore, did not agree with his late boss's policies. Fillmore fired Taylor's entire cabinet: the secretary of state, secretary of war, secretary of the treasury, and everyone else who led the executive branch. Shortly after, Fillmore pushed through the Compromise of 1850. This legislation delayed the Civil War by a decade but couldn't stop it forever.

MILLARD FILLMORE

"God knows I detest slavery, but it is an existing evil . . . and we must endure it and give it such protection as is guaranteed by the constitution."

Millard Fillmore, letter to his secretary of state, October 23, 1850

NEWS NATIONAL

The World in 1850

Zachary Taylor died four months before this message to Congress, leaving America with an unlucky thirteenth president: Millard Fillmore. Fillmore hadn't gotten much face time with his late boss, and few Americans knew who Millard Fillmore was. Most Americans alive today still don't know much about him!

Fillmore is a mostly forgotten president. But he had the biggest job in the country at a critical moment in United States history. The issues of the day were still slavery and westward expansion. Before his death, Zachary Taylor—an enslaver who nonetheless opposed the expansion of slavery into the western territories—had been bargaining with Congress over a deal called the Compromise of 1850. A lot was at stake: admitting California as a state, establishing the borders of Texas and New Mexico, passing the Fugitive Slave Act, and deciding the future of the slave trade in Washington, DC. Any one of these issues might tear the country apart. Taken together, they were a powder keg that could blow the United States into civil war.

As it was written, Taylor may have vetoed the entire compromise. But he wasn't around anymore. Millard Fillmore was in charge, and he pushed the compromise over the finish line by making deals with the pro-slavery side of Congress, allowing slavery to expand into the new territories.

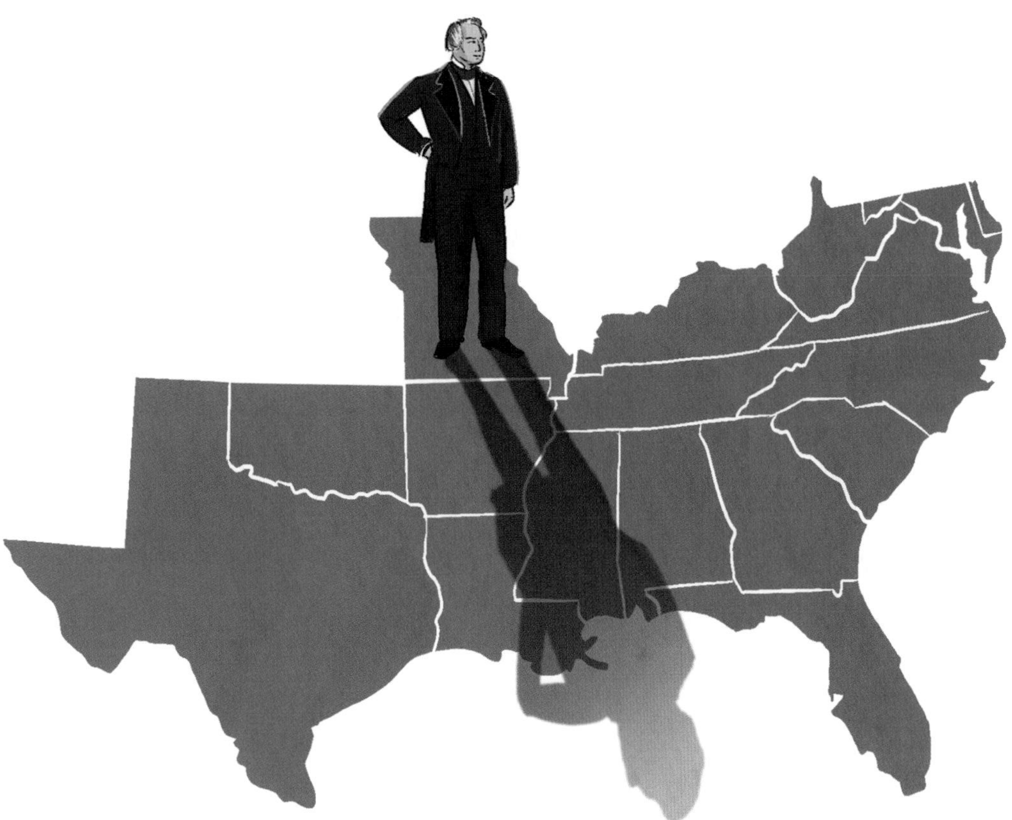

Words Have a Purpose

Fillmore was personally opposed to slavery, but he did think that the Constitution allowed it to exist and even expand to new states. He also had mixed feelings about the Compromise of 1850—as did his party, the Whigs. The pro-slavery faction wanted more slave states. And the anti-slavery faction hated the new Fugitive Slave Act, which legalized the forced return of formerly enslaved individuals who'd escaped to freedom in the North to their enslavers in the South. Congress was divided when it came to slavery.

For the new president, preserving the Union and sticking by the Constitution mattered more than anything else. He believed that the Compromise of 1850 could keep the country together—at least for now—so he was going to push for the deal to pass Congress, no matter how many messy feelings accompanied it.

Words Make a Difference

The Compromise of 1850 did settle some issues. California was admitted as a free state. Texas's boundaries were set. New Mexico became a territory. A new Fugitive Slave Act was passed, favoring the Southern states. And the slave trade in Washington, DC, was abolished.

But the fate of slavery in the United States was far from settled. The Compromise of 1850 postponed the Civil War for ten years, but most Americans still feared that a war was coming.

DID YOU KNOW?

After leaving the White House, Millard Fillmore ran for president again in 1856, this time as a leader of the Know-Nothing Party. It was an anti-immigrant, anti-Catholic group. Fillmore finished the election in third place, with just 21.6 percent of the vote.

★ ★ ★

FRANKLIN PIERCE

"The storm of frenzy and faction must inevitably dash itself in vain against the unshaken rock of the Constitution."

Franklin Pierce, Third Annual Message to Congress, December 31, 1855

The World in 1855

The Northern and Southern states were becoming even more divided over slavery, and it was clear by now that the Compromise of 1850 could not keep the country together. Franklin Pierce was from New Hampshire, a free state. But the northerner wasn't always on the North's side in these debates. In fact, he agreed with the Southern states much of the time.

In 1854, the new Kansas-Nebraska Act—which Pierce had supported—passed Congress. Today, most people have forgotten about Franklin Pierce, but the Kansas-Nebraska Act was one of the most important laws of the nineteenth century. It got rid of the Missouri Compromise and created two new territories: Kansas and Nebraska. As always, the question was whether slavery would be allowed in either one. The Kansas-Nebraska Act left this decision up to the voters—a concept known as "popular sovereignty." The fate of slavery in the United States was on the line (as was the future balance of power in the Senate, since every new state got two new senators). Things were about to get violent in Kansas and Nebraska.

Words Have a Purpose

Nebraska was the northern of the two territories, making it more likely that voters there would oppose slavery. But Kansas looked like it would be up for grabs. So supporters on both sides moved to the new territories in droves, trying to get the votes on slavery to go their way. "Border ruffians" from Missouri squared off against "free-staters," forming pro- and anti-slavery voting blocs. There were mobs, riots, violence, and even killings. The fighting lasted for several years—becoming known as "Bleeding Kansas"—and confirmed for many that a larger armed conflict over slavery was bound to happen before long.

In his address, Franklin Pierce responded to these events, which he called a "storm of frenzy and faction." He referred to the Constitution as an "unshaken rock" because it had held the country together for nearly seven decades. Pierce hoped that the storm in Kansas would pass just as the storms over other issues had before.

Bleeding Kansas

Words Make a Difference

This storm, however, was more like a tornado. Bleeding Kansas lasted throughout Pierce's single term in office. The debates in Congress got so intense that some members even attacked each other on the Senate floor. And Pierce's popularity went down the tubes. His own party, the Democrats, refused to renominate him in the election of 1856, picking James Buchanan from Pennsylvania instead. Franklin Pierce left Washington and went back home. And the nation edged closer and closer to a civil war.

DID YOU KNOW?

Franklin Pierce's inaugural address was *really* long, clocking in at more than three thousand words! In it, he spoke about the importance of keeping the country together, saying that states should have their own rights while still remaining united. Pierce delivered the entire speech from memory, without reading from any notes. He was the first president to do that!

JAMES BUCHANAN

"I feel that my duty has been faithfully, though it may be imperfectly, performed, and, whatever the result may be, I shall carry to my grave the consciousness that I at least meant well for my country."

James Buchanan, Special Message to Congress, January 8, 1861

The World in 1861

James Buchanan's presidency was a failure. He was about to hand his successor, Abraham Lincoln, a mess. Buchanan had tried to resolve the issue of Bleeding Kansas, but the situation wasn't settled. The Supreme Court issued its awful, pro-slavery ruling in the *Dred Scott* case in 1857, which said that formerly enslaved people got no protections, even if they escaped to the North, and that Washington couldn't stop slavery from spreading to new territories.

With so much division, new political parties were forming and existing parties were changing. Even the old Democratic Party—which up to that point had traditionally been more pro-slavery—was split between Northern and Southern factions. Abraham Lincoln, a one-term former congressman from Illinois, won the November 1860 election at the head of a new, anti-slavery party: the Republicans. The Civil War was about to begin.

Words Have a Purpose

By January 1861, James Buchanan had become what's known as a "lame duck": someone who has just a few months left in office, and whose replacement has already been chosen by the voters. Lame ducks don't have a lot of power; everyone knows they'll be gone before too long.

Never an effective president, Buchanan still had two months left in office. Faced with an impending civil war, he basically just gave up. Southern states began to secede, and he let them go. Southern members of his cabinet—and of Congress—left Washington and went back home, knowing they'd be fighting against the North soon. He didn't stop them. By early February—while Buchanan was still president—seven states had left the Union. They were forming a new country that they called the Confederate States of America. When he delivered this message on January 8, 1861, Buchanan knew he had failed to keep the United States united.

Words Make a Difference

America had avoided—or at least delayed—a civil war for decades. Many presidents had tried to stop it by making compromises, even if this meant allowing slavery to continue and spread. But those compromises couldn't hold.

America had changed since George Washington's presidency. The country had grown, fought multiple wars, expanded across North America, and more—all while the issue of slavery remained unresolved. Buchanan couldn't hold back the Civil War. And he didn't really try, because he wouldn't stand up to the Southern states when they started to secede. Though he may have meant well, when it came to the president's most important job—keeping the United States united—Buchanan wasn't up to the task.

James Buchanan was the only president who never got married. Because all the presidents who *did* marry before him had had wives who took the title of first lady, this meant that America didn't have a first lady while Buchanan was in office. Instead, his niece Harriet Lane Johnston stepped in and filled the role.

ABRAHAM LINCOLN

"Four score and seven years ago our fathers brought forth on this continent a new nation, conceived in liberty, and dedicated to the proposition that all men are created equal."

Abraham Lincoln, Gettysburg Address, November 19, 1863

The World in 1863

The Civil War was the deadliest conflict in American history. The country was at war with itself—the free Northern states (the Union) against the slave-holding Southern states (the Confederacy). The fighting started in April 1861, with the Battle of Fort Sumter. The Union performed badly at first. But after victory in the three-day Battle of Gettysburg in July 1863, the Union turned the tide in the Civil War.

Four months after the battle, Abraham Lincoln headed to Gettysburg to dedicate a cemetery for the fallen. Lincoln was a wartime president—and even though the Union had won the battle, that victory came at a terrible cost. America's citizens were grieving. Lincoln needed to rally the country, honor the dead, and explain what their sacrifices were for. If he delivered a rousing speech, the Union would be even more motivated to keep fighting and win the Civil War.

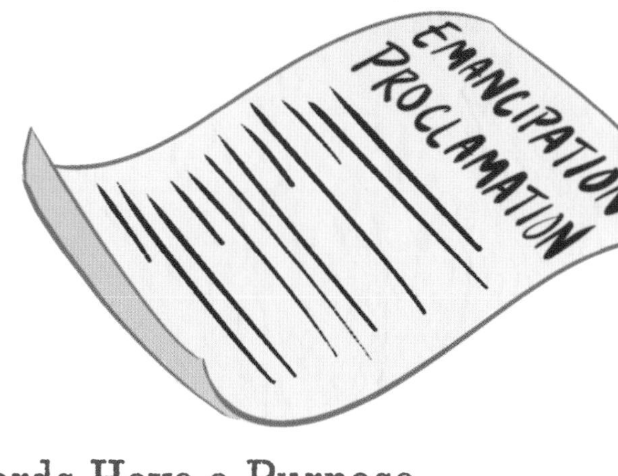

16

Words Have a Purpose

The Gettysburg Address is arguably the most famous speech ever given by an American president. It's also pretty short, clocking in at just three paragraphs, ten sentences, and 272 words. The first thing you'll notice is some math in the opening line: "Four score and seven years ago." A score is an approximate unit of measurement, meaning about twenty. When Lincoln said "four score and seven years," he was referring to a moment eighty-seven years prior: America's founding in 1776.

Lincoln put the Gettysburg Address in conversation with the Declaration of Independence to remind his audience that America was uniquely founded on the "proposition" that *every* person is equal—an ideal contradicted by the inhumane practice of slavery. The Civil War, Lincoln said, was a "test" of whether the United States could last as it was "conceived" by the Founding Fathers, flawed as they were. Lincoln believed that America could pass this test and live up to its founding principles as one unified country, without slavery. He'd issued the Emancipation Proclamation earlier that year, freeing enslaved people in states that had seceded—and by the war's end, nearly 10 percent of the Union's troops were Black men fighting for freedom.

DID YOU KNOW?

Abraham Lincoln wasn't the only speaker at Gettysburg that blustery November day. A famous orator named Edward Everett spoke for two hours before Lincoln's two-minute address. Everett was supposed to steal the show! But Lincoln proved that a speech doesn't need to be long to be memorable.

Words Make a Difference

Lincoln's speech at Gettysburg rallied not only his audience but the entire nation. He went on to win reelection in 1864, and a year later, the Union won the Civil War when Confederate General Robert E. Lee surrendered to Union General Ulysses S. Grant at Virginia's Appomattox Court House on April 9, 1865. Without Lincoln's leadership, this victory could easily have gone the other way. The war could have ended with the United States being divided forever.

Abraham Lincoln saved the Union. But on April 14, 1865, Confederate sympathizer John Wilkes Booth assassinated the president at Ford's Theater in Washington, DC. Lincoln would not live long enough to bring the country together after the war.

ANDREW JOHNSON

"*Let them impeach and be damned.*"

Andrew Johnson, upon news of his impeachment, February 1868

The World in 1868

The Civil War was over! The Union won, and slavery was abolished. But now the country had to come together again. This was a political mess—and Abraham Lincoln wasn't around to clean it up.

After Lincoln's assassination, his vice president—a former senator and enslaver from Tennessee—became president. Three years into his term, it was obvious that Andrew Johnson was *very* different from Lincoln, and in all the wrong ways. Johnson was extremely lenient toward the former Confederacy. He pardoned tens of thousands of former Confederate officeholders and let many of them lead local and state governments in the South. He also allowed new laws called "Black codes" to discriminate against formerly enslaved Black people. The era of Reconstruction, in which the seceded Southern states were rejoining the country, was off to a rocky start—and even though formerly enslaved Black Americans were now free, their treatment was often far from equal.

Lincoln's Republican Party was not happy with Johnson. Members of Congress who wanted to protect civil rights and punish the Southern states who'd seceded, were furious. In 1868, they made a big push to impeach him.

17

Words Have a Purpose

Andrew Johnson never had many friends in Washington. And those he'd once had, he was losing quickly. Johnson's fight with Congress came to a head when he fired the secretary of war, whom Lincoln had appointed and who had many powerful friends on Capitol Hill. With this move, Johnson was daring the House of Representatives to impeach him. And on February 24, 1868, the House did just that, by a vote of 126 to 47.

Impeaching a president is complicated. First, the House takes a majority vote on the articles of impeachment, which describe what the president is being impeached for. The Constitution says the president can be impeached for "Treason, Bribery, or other high Crimes and Misdemeanors." After a majority vote to impeach, there's a trial in the Senate. The president can only be removed from office if two-thirds of the senators vote in favor—a high bar.

Words Make a Difference

Johnson's impeachment trial was a huge public spectacle. There were dozens of witnesses and tons of press. The final Senate vote was a nail-biter. The result was thirty-five votes in favor of removal, with just nineteen against. But this result was still one vote shy of the two-thirds needed to kick Johnson out. Johnson would remain president until his term ended on March 4, 1869.

Andrew Johnson isn't remembered fondly, but he had once seemed like a great choice for Lincoln's vice president. He was the only Southern senator who stayed loyal to the Union, which made him a hero to many Americans. In 1864, Lincoln replaced his former vice president with Johnson because he thought the Tennessee senator would help bring the country together.

ULYSSES S. GRANT

"The war is over; the rebels are our countrymen again."

Ulysses S. Grant, upon accepting General Robert E. Lee's surrender at Appomattox Court House, April 9, 1865

The World in 1865

Grant was the general who won the Civil War for the Union. It was not an easy fight. When the battles were over, more than six hundred thousand Americans had lost their lives, and much of the South lay in ruins. By April 1865, the only thing left was for the Confederacy to formally surrender.

On April 9, 1865, at Appomattox Court House, Confederate General Robert E. Lee and his Army of Northern Virginia finally surrendered to Union General Ulysses S. Grant. With Lee off the battlefield, the remaining Confederates couldn't hold out much longer. What came next was anyone's guess. Uniting the country after so much destruction would take a lot of work. The fight for full equality of formerly enslaved people—and for all Black Americans—was far from over.

18

Words Have a Purpose

When General Lee surrendered at Appomattox Court House, many northerners wanted to celebrate, and maybe seek revenge. They'd just won a long and difficult war, and they were getting ready to throw their hats in the air and shoot off their cannons to mark the occasion. Many did not think that the South should be welcomed back with open arms.

But Grant had a different perspective. He didn't think that celebrating was a good idea, or that punishing the Confederates was the right way to go. He'd won the war for the Union, but now he had to win the peace for the entire United States. This meant ensuring that his troops started to see the rebels as fellow Americans again, and that the old Confederates rejoined their country in good faith. Grant was generous to Lee during the surrender ceremony—an example he continued to set after he was elected president in 1868.

Words Make a Difference

After the Civil War, Americans needed to find a way to live together again. This was no easy task. The states' divisions on race, federalism, and so much else were very real. The Civil War had proved how deep these divisions were—and though the fighting was over, they hadn't gone away.

Grant's generosity toward Lee at Appomattox Court House set an example for the entire country. There's no telling what might have happened if he'd tried to punish or humiliate Lee. Would the rebels continue fighting? Would the war resume in just a few years? Could Northern and Southern states ever come together in a union that would last? Grant worried about all these questions, and ultimately, he decided that the best way to move forward as one united country was to be gracious in victory. No gloating, no revenge. Just reconciliation.

Ulysses S. Grant's first name wasn't always Ulysses. He had been born Hiram Ulysses Grant—HUG—and other boys sometimes teased him about his initials. But later in life, he went by Ulysses S. Grant, and his supporters joked that his first two initials now stood for "Unconditional Surrender."

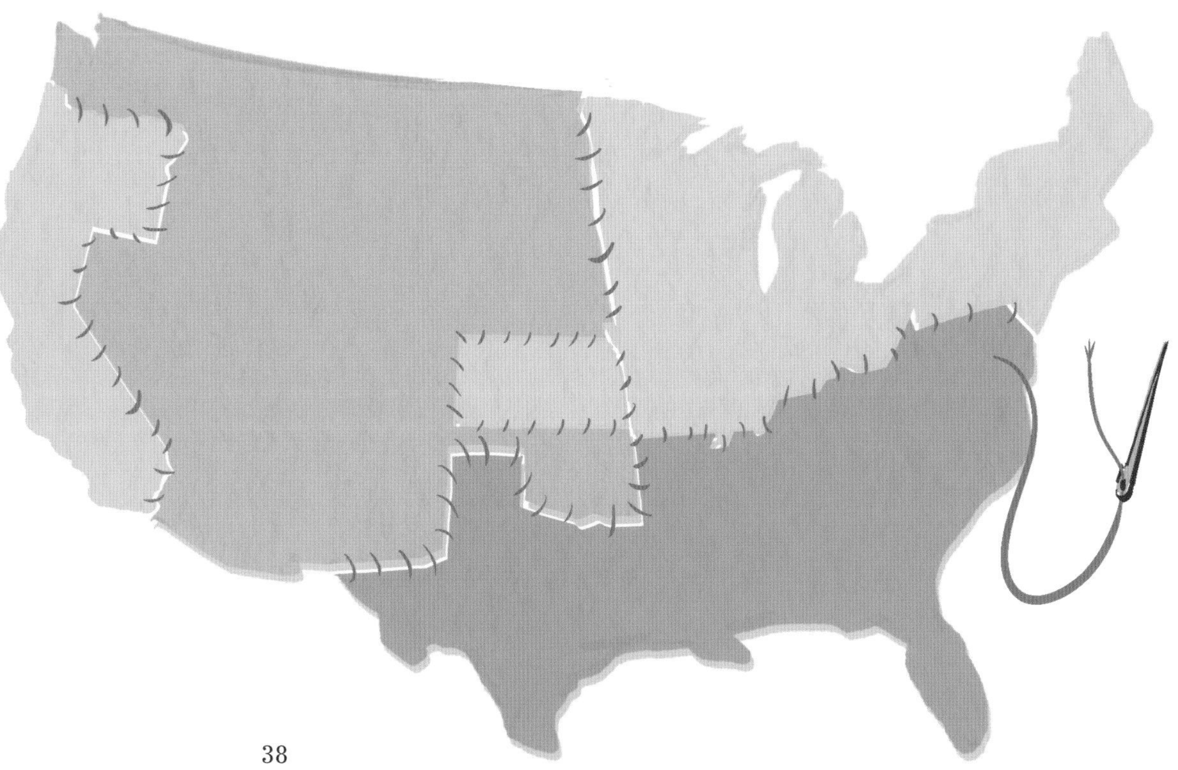

RUTHERFORD B. HAYES

"It is the desire of the good people of the whole country that sectionalism as a factor in our politics should disappear."

Rutherford B. Hayes, Fourth Annual Message to Congress, December 6, 1880

The World in 1880

The biggest debates of the nineteenth century were changing. Slavery was abolished, and the frontier—the western edge of land reached by American settlers—was almost gone. Reconstruction formally ended in 1877, when federal troops left the South. At the same time, the United States was urbanizing, with more people moving to the cities for work and new groups of immigrants coming to America.

Politics was still chaotic. The last three presidencies had not gone according to plan. Abraham Lincoln had been assassinated—a first in American history. Andrew Johnson had been impeached—another first. The Grant administration had plenty of scandals of its own. After all that, the American people wanted stability. After a close election in 1876, they got it with Rutherford B. Hayes. The new president had a lot of work ahead of him.

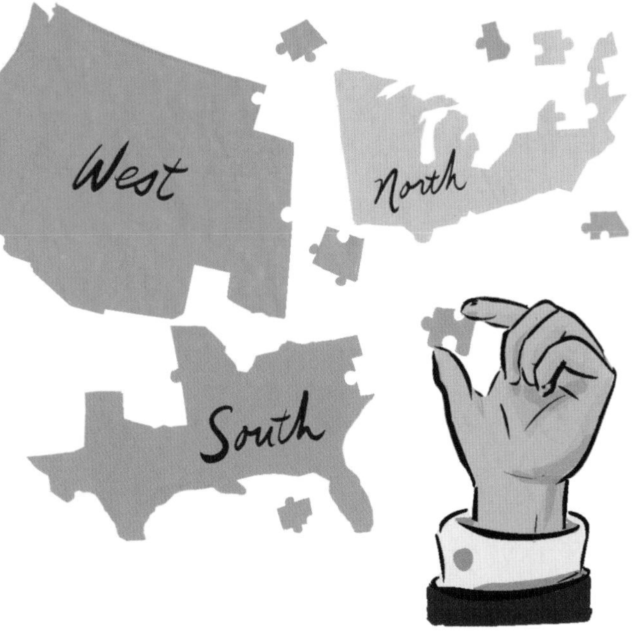

Words Have a Purpose

Politics can be very divisive. During his final address to Congress, Hayes spoke about "sectionalism." Sectionalism pits Americans against each other along geographic, religious, racial, or any number of other lines. In a democratic republic, citizens have different opinions, and they sort out those differences at the ballot box. But during the Civil War, America had seen what happens when sectionalism gets out of hand, with the country literally splitting into two (Northern states versus Southern states) and going to war with itself. Even once the war was over, "sectionalism" persisted. The country was divided.

With Reconstruction in the rearview mirror, Hayes was trying to bring the newly reunited country together. He assured his audience that the United States could move beyond the regional divisions that had been the biggest factor in its politics for decades.

Words Make a Difference

Rutherford B. Hayes sent his final address—what today we'd call his State of the Union—to Congress in 1880. He was pretty satisfied. The country he would leave to his successor was, he thought, "united, harmonious, and prosperous." Of course, there were still huge issues—particularly in the South, where Black Americans were often denied their rights and discriminatory Jim Crow laws were taking hold. But slavery was no more. The economy was growing. And the United States was more stable on the whole than it had been when Hayes took over.

DID YOU KNOW?

In the 1876 election, Republican Rutherford B. Hayes won the presidency against Democrat Samuel J. Tilden. This was one of the closest elections in American history, and the results weren't finalized on Election Day. Congress had to form a special commission in January—two months after the voting took place—to figure out who had won. After much deliberation, the commission awarded Hayes the disputed votes from Louisiana, South Carolina, and Florida, making him the nineteenth president of the United States.

JAMES A. GARFIELD

"The elevation of the [Black] race from slavery to the full rights of citizenship is the most important political change we have known since the adoption of the Constitution of 1787."

James A. Garfield, Inaugural Address, March 4, 1881

The World in 1881

James A. Garfield had won the 1880 election, but by just a few thousand votes. Despite the close results, Garfield was an inspiring figure. Born in a log cabin in Ohio, his humble beginnings gave hope to poor Americans. And both Black Americans and former abolitionists warmed to him, since Garfield had long been on their side.

Garfield's ambitions for his presidency and the country included civil service reform for the federal government and civil rights for Black Americans. He wanted to get rid of corrupt party politics where jobs went to the well-connected, not the well-qualified—an arrangement known as the "spoils system."

Unfortunately, Garfield wouldn't get to see his plans through. Just 120 days after his inauguration, Garfield was shot by an assassin. He became the fourth American president to die in office, and the second to be killed.

Words Have a Purpose

Inaugural addresses are often the most important speeches that a president ever gives. They set the tone for the presidency. Each president gets to give just one inaugural address—or, if they're lucky and win reelection, maybe two. Garfield chose to do two big things in his first (and only) inaugural address. First, he reflected on the Civil War, reminding the country what a historic accomplishment it was to finally abolish slavery in the United States. And second, he took stock of the work that still needed to be done, especially on pressing civil rights issues, at a time when racial segregation was the law of the land in many Southern states.

Garfield cared about suffrage (meaning the right to vote). Following the end of Reconstruction in 1876, many Black Americans were still not allowed to exercise their "full rights of citizenship" at the ballot box. This wasn't supposed to happen—especially since the Fifteenth Amendment to the Constitution explicitly stated that American citizens *couldn't* be denied their right to vote on the basis of race. But state governments in the South were making it impossible for Black Americans, and a lot of poor southerners, to vote. They used policies like literacy tests and poll taxes to deny citizens their rights. In his first speech as president, Garfield planted his flag firmly in the camp of civil rights.

Words Make a Difference

The fight for equality wasn't new to Garfield. But what *was* new was his much bigger platform in the White House. Garfield's inaugural address argued that civil rights for Black Americans were a fundamental aspect of striving for a more perfect union—consistent with the ideals on which the United States was founded. But sadly, Garfield's assassination deprived America of one of its great civil rights champions.

DID YOU KNOW?

James A. Garfield was a lifelong champion of rights for Black Americans. As a young boy in Ohio, he helped hide a runaway slave who was escaping north along the Underground Railroad to freedom in Canada.

CHESTER A. ARTHUR

"There are very many characteristics which go to making a model civil servant. Prominent among them are probity, industry, good sense, good habits, good temper, patience, order, courtesy, tact, self-reliance, manly deference to superior officers, and manly consideration for inferiors."

Chester A. Arthur, First Annual Message to Congress, December 6, 1881

The World in 1881

Politics can be an honorable profession, but it's often a dirty business. Politicians don't always have great reputations. Under the so-called "spoils system," government jobs didn't go to the most qualified candidates. Instead, they went to people with friends in the right places. This practice was normal for both major political parties, the Democrats and the Republicans.

Voters were outraged by political scandals and corruption. Political parties kept rewarding the same old party bosses and loyalists. And Ulysses S. Grant had left office in 1877 with a cloud of suspicion hanging over his head. When Chester A. Arthur became president in 1881, after Garfield's death, it looked like nothing would change. After all, he was very much a part of that spoils system. But this impression turned out to be wrong!

Words Have a Purpose

Civil servants are the people employed to keep the government running. They manage America's post offices, ports, emergency services, and everything in between. These are important jobs, and they're not supposed to be political. But under the spoils system, they weren't always going to people who could do them well based on their skills, education, or other qualifications.

Chester A. Arthur was an unlikely champion for civil service reform. But after Garfield's assassination, he took up the cause with gusto. When he went through the characteristics that he believed made a good civil servant, his list wasn't about politics or connections. It was about character and competence: what kind of person you are, and what you can do.

21

Words Make a Difference

Arthur enacted the biggest reforms to civil service in American history, known as the Pendleton Civil Service Act. Government employees no longer had to donate to or participate in political parties to get their jobs. After 1883, a competitive, merit-based system for government jobs was enacted, doing away with the old spoils system and using exams to determine whether candidates were qualified for the jobs.

☞ DID YOU KNOW?

As vice president, Arthur was devastated when he learned that James A. Garfield had been shot. He told the cabinet, "I pray to God that the President will recover. God knows I do not want the place I was never elected to." After Garfield was shot, Arthur tried to visit his boss's bedside. But he was not allowed in.

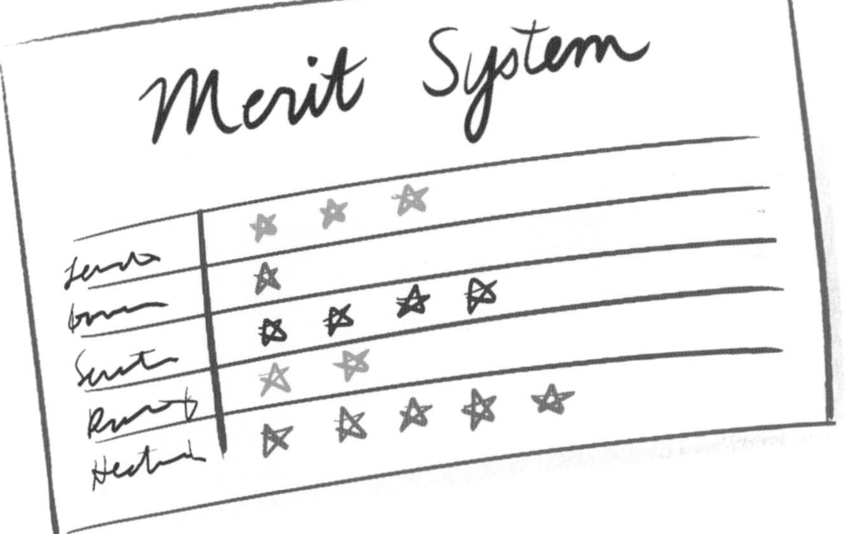

GROVER CLEVELAND

"What is the use of being elected or reelected unless you stand for something?"

Grover Cleveland, on his refusal to compromise on tariff reform, December 1887

The World in 1887

Grover Cleveland was elected president in 1884, becoming the first Democratic president to win the White House since the Civil War. Now Cleveland was running for reelection, and the question was whether the American people would grant him a second term in the country's highest office.

TARIFF REFORM ☆ PUBLIC OFFICE IS A PUBLIC TRUST

The main issue of the day was the matter of tariffs. Tariffs are taxes that the federal government charges on imports, or goods coming to the United States from other countries. Cleveland was against high tariffs because he thought they were unnecessary, and that they'd hurt American farmers. But business owners who didn't want to compete against foreign manufacturers liked tariffs. This debate may seem nerdy, but tariffs were a big deal then—and sometimes they are even today.

Cleveland knew how divisive the tariff issue was. If he vetoed a big tariff bill in 1887, it could cost him the presidency in 1888. But he'd run for president to get the job done, and he wanted to make decisions he believed in.

22 & 24

Words Have a Purpose

Cleveland's political allies tried to get him to allow the tariff to go through. They told him he'd need to compromise to stay in power. But with this rhetorical question, Cleveland was letting his aides know that he wasn't going to change his mind about a policy just because it might benefit him politically. He believed he was doing the right thing. And now it would be up to the voters to decide if they wanted to give him another term.

Words Make a Difference

Grover Cleveland stuck by his principles, no matter the political costs. He lost his reelection to Republican Benjamin Harrison in 1888. But the American people hadn't given up on him. He'd actually won more of the popular vote than Harrison, even though he lost the Electoral College tally. (The Electoral College is used to choose America's presidents: Citizens in each state vote on which candidate they want their state's electors to support, with each state getting the same number of electors as it has members of Congress. Whichever candidate gets a majority of votes in the Electoral College wins.)

Cleveland was set up for a comeback in 1892. The economy was a mess, and the American people were ready to give Cleveland another chance. Because he stuck with his principles, they trusted him, and they sent him back to the White House.

DID YOU KNOW?

Grover Cleveland was both America's twenty-second and twenty-fourth president. He won the presidency in 1884 and lost his bid for reelection in 1888. But he ran again—and won!—in 1892. Cleveland ended up serving two terms, but they were nonconsecutive, meaning they didn't happen one right after the other. He's the only person in American history to pull this off.

BENJAMIN HARRISON

"It is essential that none of the other great powers shall secure these islands [Hawai'i]. Such a possession would not consist with our safety and with the peace of the world."

Benjamin Harrison, Message to the Senate Transmitting a Treaty to Annex the Hawaiian Islands, February 15, 1893

The World in 1893

President Benjamin Harrison was on his way out of the White House. He had just lost his bid for reelection to Grover Cleveland. And he was leaving several big messes on his successor's desk. One of the biggest issues was far away, on a few beautiful islands in the Pacific Ocean.

America was now a Pacific power with a growing navy. The Hawaiian Islands (then an independent country known as the Kingdom of Hawai'i) were becoming more important every day. They were located in the middle of the Pacific Ocean, and many US officials and businesspeople felt they were the perfect place for ships to refuel during long journeys; for Christian missionaries to spread the Gospel; and—maybe most importantly—for sugarcane production.

But the vast majority of Native Hawaiians weren't happy about the increased US presence near their homes. Tensions were high, and in 1893, American settlers staged a coup to depose Hawaiian Queen Lili'uokalani and take the islands by force. These American forces didn't act under direction from Washington—they just took over! Whether or not its people wanted to, it looked like Hawai'i would shortly become part of the United States.

Words Have a Purpose

Benjamin Harrison spoke for a powerful group of Americans who wanted the United States to play a more active role on the world stage. Some were imperialists, because they wanted the US to take new territories abroad. Other Americans thought this approach was wrong, especially since the United States was founded after winning its own independence from an empire.

Harrison certainly didn't want European countries to take over the Hawaiian Islands, because that would threaten the United States' hold in the Pacific and thus, in his view, the "peace of the world." He pushed for the United States to annex Hawai'i (a move that the deposed Queen Lili'uokalani fiercely opposed), and he also allowed US Marines to keep the provisional government in power, over the objections of Native Hawaiians. When it came to Hawai'i, America was acting like an empire.

Words Make a Difference

The president cannot just annex new territory on his own. In order for Hawai'i to become part of the United States, Harrison needed the Senate to approve a treaty. He sent one to the Senate in the final days of his presidency. But the Senate didn't have time to get to it before he left office.

Unlike Harrison, Grover Cleveland didn't want to annex Hawai'i. He ordered Queen Lili'uokalani restored to power and removed the treaty from the Senate's consideration. But when Cleveland left office, the Senate approved a new annexation treaty. And Hawai'i became a territory of the United States in 1898.

DID YOU KNOW?

The Hawaiian Islands were once called the "Sandwich Islands" by people not native to the islands. This wasn't because they had particularly good sandwiches—it was because an eighteenth-century explorer named them after the British Earl of Sandwich.

WILLIAM MCKINLEY

"War should never be entered upon until every agency of peace has failed; peace is preferable to war in almost every contingency."

William McKinley, First Inaugural Address, March 4, 1897

The World in 1897

William McKinley was president, and many Americans were ready to go to war. They had their eyes trained on an island just a few miles off the coast of Florida, where Cuban rebels were fighting for freedom from the colonial Spanish Empire.

Americans were watching what was happening in Cuba very closely. They worried that any instability in Cuba could spread to the rest of the Caribbean. At the same time, many wanted the Cuban rebels to win. America had won its Revolutionary War against the British Empire, and Americans supported the independence movement. A lot of voters wanted the United States to declare war on Spain, taking the side of the Cuban rebels. But when he took office, William McKinley promised to stay neutral and keep the country out of war.

Words Have a Purpose

William McKinley knew that the American public would support him if he went to war with Spain. But, at least for now, he was promising to keep America out of the conflict in Cuba.

For the first year of McKinley's presidency, America remained neutral. This was in keeping with a policy of staying out of foreign wars that went back decades, all the way to George Washington's farewell address. But even if McKinley believed that peace was preferable to war, he wouldn't be able to *keep* the peace for long.

Words Make a Difference

At a certain point, there was little the president could say that would keep America out of the war. The relationship between the United States and the Spanish Empire was going downhill. Spain was abusing the Cuban people. And at the same time, the US was growing stronger, steadily asserting its power in the Caribbean. On February 15, 1898, when the USS *Maine* (an American battleship) exploded and then sank to the bottom of Cuba's Havana Harbor, war started to look inevitable.

The explosion on the *Maine* may have been an accident. But it was an excuse for war with the Spanish Empire. Two months later, the United States took the Cuban rebels' side and declared the start of the Spanish-American War. After just four months of fighting, the United States won, even though the treaty wouldn't be officially signed until December of that year. It took control of Puerto Rico, Guam, and the Philippines from Spain, and Cuba became an independent country.

William McKinley had a pet parrot! Its name was Washington Post. McKinley's parrot was pretty patriotic—it could whistle "Yankee Doodle."

THEODORE ROOSEVELT

"It is not the critic who counts; not the man who points out how the strong man stumbles or where the doer of deeds could have done them better. The credit belongs to the man who is actually in the arena. . . ."

Theodore Roosevelt, Address at the Sorbonne in Paris, France: "Citizenship in a Republic," April 23, 1910

The World in 1910

The United States had never had a president quite like Theodore ("TR" or "Teddy") Roosevelt. He was a force of nature! Though he'd been very sick as a child, Roosevelt became a talented athlete who rode horses, swam, wrestled, and hunted big game such as lions, elephants, and rhinoceroses. He was a hero from the Spanish-American War. He would go on to change the presidency forever, vastly expanding the people's understanding of what a president could do.

The American people loved Roosevelt. His charisma and decisive action made him popular, and sometimes controversial. He pushed for environmental conservation, regulation of big business, and welfare programs. He demonstrated to the world that America was a force to be reckoned with, sending a fleet of US Navy battleships (all painted white) around the globe. By the time Roosevelt left the White House in 1909, his reputation was sky-high. Even though he could have won, he didn't run for another term, deciding instead to hand the presidency over to his chosen successor, William Howard Taft. But by 1910, Theodore Roosevelt wanted to be president again.

Words Have a Purpose

Roosevelt was a powerful public speaker, popularizing a term called the "bully pulpit" to describe the platform of the presidency. He encouraged others to be as daring as he was, urging them to throw themselves fully into whatever pursuit they were undertaking.

Part of Roosevelt's passion came from the health struggles he endured in his childhood. He'd been sick a lot as a boy, and he had bad asthma. But he discovered that physical activity improved his symptoms, and he became determined to live a full and active life. His speech in Paris celebrated virtues like persistence and determination, as well as the American spirit. Maybe he should have known that he wouldn't be able to just retire from the presidency and live out his days quietly—he always wanted to be in the arena.

Words Make a Difference

Roosevelt was no longer the president when he made his remarks about the "man in the arena." But he was still one of the most popular Americans alive, and he knew he could run for president again in 1912 if he wanted. He was disappointed by the policies of his successor, William Howard Taft, who was more conservative than Roosevelt.

So Roosevelt ran for president again in 1912, when Taft's first term was up. It was a four-way race, with Roosevelt and Taft splitting the Republican vote and a socialist candidate named Eugene V. Debs also having a strong showing. The winner, Democratic candidate Woodrow Wilson, earned enough support in the Electoral College to head to the White House, even without a majority of the popular votes.

Theodore Roosevelt won the Nobel Peace Prize in 1906 for his role mediating the end of the Russo-Japanese War, which lasted from 1904 to 1905. Roosevelt was the first American president to win a Nobel.

WILLIAM HOWARD TAFT

"I love judges, and I love courts. They are my ideals that typify on earth what we shall meet hereafter in heaven under a just God."

William Howard Taft, reflecting on the Supreme Court, October 1911

The World in 1911

William Howard Taft didn't really want to be president. He wanted to be a Supreme Court justice! But his family had pushed him to run for the White House, and Theodore Roosevelt had chosen him as his successor. While First Lady Nellie Taft was happy to be in Washington, DC, her husband wanted to leave the White House behind.

Taft was a different kind of president from Roosevelt. Whereas Roosevelt expanded the power of the presidency to new limits, Taft believed that if the Constitution didn't explicitly say a president could do something, then he couldn't do it. This is a theory of constitutional, limited government.

27

Words Have a Purpose

William Howard Taft wasn't shy about letting people know that he loved the courts more than the White House. He came from a family of lawyers—and his father, Alphonso Taft, was Ulysses S. Grant's attorney general. William Howard Taft had been a federal judge, as well as the solicitor general of the United States! Taft loved being a judge—hearing arguments, debating them with his colleagues, making a ruling about which side was right according to the law, and staying out of politics.

Taft had been offered a job on the Supreme Court at least three times before he became president. But he'd had to turn each opportunity down because the timing just wasn't right. Now, after having served as president, he was surer than ever that he was meant to be on the court and not in the White House.

Words Make a Difference

Taft lost the 1912 election. It looked like his career in Washington might be over. Few former presidents ever run for office again (Grover Cleveland aside). And none had ever been appointed to the Supreme Court. But then Warren G. Harding was elected president in 1920, and Taft got another shot at his dream job.

Harding liked Taft—they were both Republicans from Ohio, and Taft was one of the sharpest legal minds of his generation. So the new president appointed Taft to the Supreme Court. Not only that, Harding made Taft the chief justice!

DID YOU KNOW?

Back in 1910, William Howard Taft did something no other president had done before: he kicked off the baseball season by tossing the first pitch! The opening game was between the Washington Senators and the Philadelphia Athletics, and the Senators won 3–0. Nearly every president since Taft has thrown at least one ceremonial first pitch.

★ ★ ★

WOODROW WILSON

"The world must be made safe for democracy. Its peace must be planted upon the tested foundations of political liberty."

Woodrow Wilson, Address to a Joint Session of Congress Requesting a Declaration of War Against Germany, April 2, 1917

The World in 1917

World War I was in its third year, and the death toll on the battlefields of Europe was unimaginably high. Under Woodrow Wilson, America had stayed out of the conflict. But the United States was about to enter the fray on the side of the Allied powers, which included the United Kingdom, France, Italy, Japan, and Russia.

The United States entered World War I for many reasons. In 1915, a German submarine sank an ocean liner called the *Lusitania*, killing 128 Americans. After a brief pause, Germany resumed unrestricted submarine warfare in February 1917, sinking ships carrying American citizens once again. The German government even wrote a secret message to Mexico—the Zimmermann Telegram—proposing that America's southern neighbor attack the United States and take control of states like Texas.

1917 was a revolutionary year. Not only did the United States enter World War I, but there was also a revolution in Russia. Russia had been ruled by an emperor (known as the czar), but the Bolsheviks—a group of communists led by a man named Vladimir Lenin—took over, and soon the Soviet Union would be born.

28

Words Have a Purpose

A former professor and university president, Wilson was an intellectual. He had bigger, more transformative ideas for when the war was over than just victory over the German military. Wilson argued that *this* war would be more than another instance of one country—or even several groups of countries—fighting another. It was a chance to establish a new world order based on ideals like democracy and self-determination.

Words Make a Difference

Four days after Wilson's address, Congress voted to declare war on Germany. It would take a while for most American troops to make it over to Europe and tip the scales against Germany. But ultimately, more than four million American soldiers would be involved in the conflict. By the time the fighting was over, more than fifty thousand had died in combat.

World War I officially ended at 11:00 a.m. on November 11, 1918. With America's help, the Allies had won. Every year, Americans mark the occasion with Veterans Day, which is called Armistice Day in much of the rest of the world.

After the war, Woodrow Wilson worked to make good on his promise. Through the peace negotiations at Versailles in France, he helped lead the creation of a new international body called the League of Nations. Even though America did not join the League, the organization laid the groundwork for the United Nations to come.

DID YOU KNOW?

In 1919, Woodrow Wilson suffered a series of awful strokes that left him too weak to perform his duties. For over a month, First Lady Edith Bolling Galt Wilson (Wilson's wife) and his doctor took over Wilson's responsibilities.

WARREN G. HARDING

"America's present need is not heroics, but healing; not nostrums, but normalcy; not revolution, but restoration."

Warren G. Harding, on the campaign trail, May 14, 1920

The World in 1920

America had just witnessed a challenging four years. Over fifty thousand Americans had died in combat during World War I, and more than ten times that many had died during the 1918 flu epidemic. Riots were gripping many cities. A series of bombings was part of the first Red Scare, in which many Americans thought the same revolutionary tide that had kicked the czar out of power in Russia would come to the United States. The economy wasn't doing well. And to top it all off, Woodrow Wilson had suffered multiple strokes and was too sick to receive visitors or perform his duties.

What Americans wanted now was a return to normalcy. And that's what Warren G. Harding promised to deliver if elected president.

29

Words Have a Purpose

Warren G. Harding tapped into the national mood perfectly in 1920. His campaign slogans and speeches talked about stability and normalcy in a time of uncertainty and upheaval. That's what Americans wanted to hear.

Woodrow Wilson was an idealist who'd made big promises. But Harding chose to build his campaign around concrete, kitchen-table issues. He promised Americans "healing" and "restoration"—in other words, that he would deliver peace, prosperity, and calm. All Americans had to do to get back to normal, he said, was vote for him.

Words Make a Difference

Warren G. Harding practically cruised into the White House in 1920. This was the first presidential election in American history in which women had the right to vote, after the passage of the Nineteenth Amendment in 1919 and its ratification in 1920. Harding won in a landslide, with more than 60 percent of the popular vote. His opponent James Cox (who ended up with a measly 34 percent of the popular vote) didn't stand a chance, even with a young man named Franklin Delano Roosevelt as his running mate.

Harding's presidency began what became known as the "Roaring Twenties," a time of peace and amazing economic growth for the United States. But despite his promises, Harding's administration was anything but normal. There would be scandals aplenty to keep the press and the people occupied. The biggest shock of all came in 1923, when Harding died of a heart attack and Vice President Calvin Coolidge took over. Under "Silent Cal," there were no big scandals, and for most Americans it really *did* feel like a return to normalcy. The Roaring Twenties kept right on roaring.

☞ DID YOU KNOW?

Presidents have always had help writing their remarks. Even George Washington had both James Madison and Alexander Hamilton help with his farewell address! But Warren G. Harding was the first president to hire an official presidential speechwriter: a man named Judson Welliver.

CALVIN COOLIDGE

"If all men are created equal, that is final. If they are endowed with inalienable rights, that is final. If governments derive their just powers from the consent of the governed, that is final. No advance, no progress can be made beyond these propositions."

Calvin Coolidge, Address at the Celebration of the 150th Anniversary of the Declaration of Independence, July 5, 1926

The World in 1926

It was America's 150th birthday, and Calvin Coolidge was in Philadelphia to celebrate. Americans were ready to party too: the economy was booming, the world was still mostly at peace, and the United States seemed like the most powerful country in the world.

Philadelphia was the perfect place for the occasion. This was where the Declaration of Independence was signed in 1776, and where the Constitution was written in 1787. An audience of two hundred thousand people was eager to hear what the president had to say. And Coolidge came bearing a powerful message: the ideals on which America was founded were true, and they were enduring. The US had more hard work ahead, but it also had a lot to look forward to. What Americans needed to do now, he said, was look back to the country's founding principles and continue striving to make them into realities.

Words Have a Purpose

The 150th anniversary of the signing of the Declaration of Independence was a great chance for the president, and the country, to reflect on all that had happened since 1776. After all, the country wasn't young anymore. Amidst all the changes and chaos at the start of the twentieth century, Coolidge reminded his audience to reflect on everything the founders got right—as well as what they didn't. For his part, Coolidge put America's founding principles into practice by focusing on limited government. His presidency was not as active as Roosevelt's and Wilson's before him; he had a more modest vision for his role.

Words Make a Difference

Presidents often return to 1776 in their speeches. That's what Abraham Lincoln did in the opening line of his Gettysburg Address, and it's what Coolidge did in 1926. Memories of the founding remind Americans of the purpose of their government, and why it was truly revolutionary. The rights of life, liberty, and the pursuit of happiness—written about in the Declaration of Independence and given a framework in the Constitution—bind Americans together even today.

There's another reason why Americans keep revisiting the founding: because the country hasn't always lived up to those ideals, especially in the beginning. The founders were far from perfect—many of them enslaved men, women, and children. And America itself will never be perfect. It has failed often, and it will fail again in the future. But the Constitution states that its purpose is to help form "a more perfect union." Not being perfect doesn't stop the American people from striving to do better, or to make good on the US's founding ideals.

DID YOU KNOW?

Calvin Coolidge's nickname was "Silent Cal." But he actually had a lot to say! Coolidge held 520 press conferences over the course of his presidency, averaging around eight a month. He was also the first president to deliver his formal addresses on the radio, and most Americans tuned in to hear. Franklin D. Roosevelt made fireside chats famous, but he owed a lot to Silent Cal's pioneering work.

HERBERT HOOVER

"We in America today are nearer to the final triumph over poverty than ever before in the history of any land."

Herbert Hoover, Acceptance Speech for the Republican Nomination, August 11, 1928

The World in 1928

Herbert Hoover was an orphan from Iowa who traveled the world and became a self-made businessman in California. He was about to become president of the United States, and many Americans were feeling optimistic. The economy was still doing well. New and exciting art and music (like jazz) were everywhere. Women were voting and taking on new jobs and new looks, with a group of young ladies called the "flappers" redefining old ways of thinking about women's roles in society. World War I had been over for a decade, and many people were hopeful that there would never be another war on that scale again.

31

Words Have a Purpose

Herbert Hoover was feeling just as optimistic as the voters. He knew that he would likely win the election, and he thought the economy would keep booming. In his campaign address, Hoover focused on "the final triumph over poverty" because, in addition to business, that had been much of his life's work up to that point. He was known around the world as the "Great Humanitarian" because he'd led American famine relief efforts during World War I, saving millions of lives—and he'd later led the federal government's recovery efforts after the Great Mississippi Flood in 1927.

The American people saw Hoover's inspiring personal story and track record of success, and they voted "yes!" Hoover won almost 60 percent of the popular vote in 1928. But unbeknownst to Hoover—and the voters—the Roaring Twenties were about to come crashing down, and many more Americans were about to fall into poverty.

Words Make a Difference

The Great Depression began in 1929, a year after Hoover's remarks. Millions of Americans lost their jobs. Banks were closing left and right. The stock market was crashing. And all the economic and social progress of the Roaring Twenties looked like it was going out the window.

The causes of the Great Depression are complex and still debated today: Was it too little economic regulation? A problem with the Federal Reserve (America's national bank)? Tariffs? Or something else? Whatever the cause, many Americans blamed Herbert Hoover. He certainly didn't prevent the Depression, and he failed to make the economic situation any better in his last three years in office.

Hoover's optimism about ending poverty seemed like nothing more than a sad memory. The country was facing tremendous hardship. Many Americans were losing their life savings. Those who lost their homes set up encampments in major cities. They called these tented cities and groups of shacks "Hoovervilles."

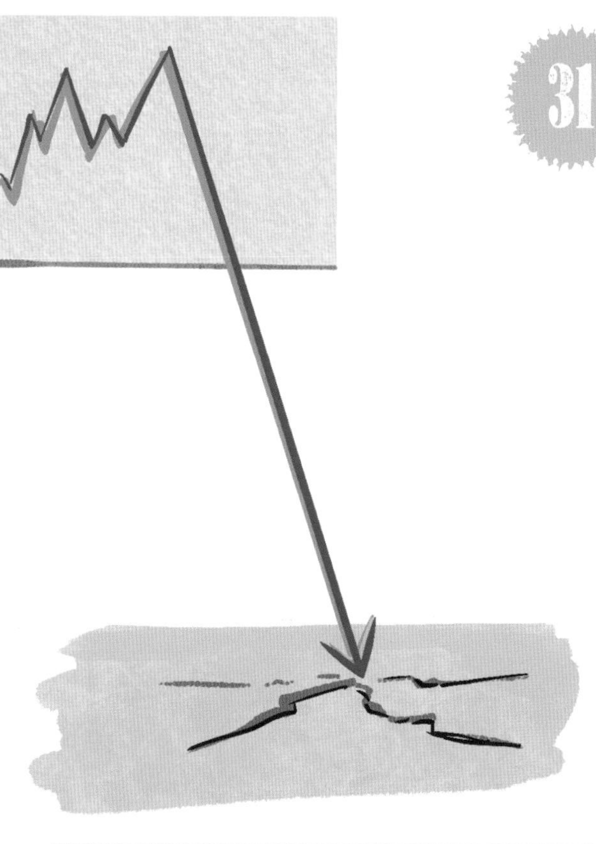

Herbert Hoover was the first president born west of the Mississippi River. He traveled the world before he entered the White House and spent some time in China during the Boxer Rebellion. He learned Mandarin while working in China as a mining engineer!

★ ★ ★

FRANKLIN D. ROOSEVELT

"The only thing we have to fear is fear itself."

Franklin D. Roosevelt, First Inaugural Address, March 4, 1933

The World in 1933

The Great Depression had dragged on for four years. More than 20 percent of the working population had lost their jobs, leaving many families without food and shelter. There was panic, desperation, and social unrest. Herbert Hoover tried to fix the economy with new agencies and new laws, but his efforts failed. Franklin D. Roosevelt (FDR) defeated Hoover in the 1932 election with a simple promise: he resolved to get America out of the Great Depression. The country believed Roosevelt was the man to do it.

Words Have a Purpose

Americans wanted a president who was charismatic and forward-looking, who could inspire them during a difficult time. Roosevelt was that man. When Roosevelt gave his speech, many Americans were desperately withdrawing their money from failing banks, which were closing in small towns and big cities alike. Roosevelt knew the country needed a confidence boost.

To help end the panic, Roosevelt believed that he needed to offer hope, to make people believe that the Depression wouldn't last forever. His masterful "freedom from fear" speech was meant to inspire. And it worked! Roosevelt's words gave the people confidence that their new president had a plan to fix the economy. If the only thing to fear was fear itself—rather than a never-ending Depression—maybe everything really would be all right.

Words Make a Difference

Franklin D. Roosevelt's words set the stage for the New Deal, a series of massive government programs addressing everything from the banks, to agriculture, to old-age pensions. Roosevelt had an unprecedented twelve years in office to push his New Deal. He led the nation through the Great Depression and—after Imperial Japan attacked Pearl Harbor on December 7, 1941 (which he called in another famous speech "a date which will live in infamy")—World War II.

Not since the Civil War had the United States faced so many existential challenges all at once. Under Roosevelt, the country began to recover. But it would be a long time before the Depression was over. Roosevelt died in office, and his successor, Harry S. Truman, finished the job.

DID YOU KNOW?

In 1921, at the age of thirty-nine, Franklin D. Roosevelt began to experience paralysis, and he was soon unable to move from the waist down. He was diagnosed with infantile paralysis, or polio. Still, Roosevelt was one of America's most active and energetic presidents, using a wheelchair and braces to move around during his entire twelve years in office.

HARRY S. TRUMAN

"I believe that it must be the policy of the United States to support free peoples who are resisting attempted subjugation by armed minorities or by outside pressures."

Harry S. Truman, "Truman Doctrine"
Address to Congress, March 12, 1947

TRUMAN DOCTRINE

The World in 1947

World War II ended in victory for the Allies (this time led by the United States, the Soviet Union, the United Kingdom, and the Republic of China) in 1945. They defeated what were known as the Axis powers: Hitler's Germany, Mussolini's Italy, and Imperial Japan.

But the world was not at peace. This was the start of what became known as the Cold War, which got its name because most of the time there was no active combat between the two great powers involved (the United States and the Soviet Union). Instead, a competition played out between the United States and other democratic countries on one side, and the Soviet Union and other communist countries on the other. The rest of the world was often caught in between. The Cold War defined United States foreign policy, and global affairs, until 1991.

33

Words Have a Purpose

Harry Truman's statement became known as the Truman Doctrine. At the time, the Soviet Union was supporting communist groups around the world as they tried to overthrow governments and create new regimes. But Truman stated that the United States would stand against that action. If there were "free people" who opposed the spread of communism in their home countries, then America would provide money, weapons, and other support to give them a fighting chance.

Truman knew that most countries were not strong enough to resist the Soviet Union on their own. Many were still rebuilding after World War II. If the United States didn't help, new communist governments hostile to the United States—and often brutal to their own people—would begin taking over. Truman started a policy of containment, under which the United States would work to stop the spread of Soviet influence. That policy set the course for the US during the Cold War and was followed by Democrats and Republicans alike.

Words Make a Difference

Before World War II, most Americans had thought that their country was safe from war. After all, the United States was bordered by two oceans and friendly neighbors. But Pearl Harbor showed that America wasn't isolated from the world's troubles—and after World War II, Truman knew that the United States would have to play a more active role in world affairs.

Under Truman, the United States sent troops to Western Europe to patrol the Soviet Union's borders. With a mandate from the newly created United Nations, American troops headed to the Korean Peninsula to protect South Korea. Later presidents sent troops and supported anti-communist forces in faraway Vietnam and nearby Cuba. There were successes as well as costly, terrible failures.

Harry Truman did not have a middle name. *S* was meant to honor both of his grandfathers: Anderson Shipp Truman and Solomon Young.

DWIGHT D. EISENHOWER

"In the councils of government, we must guard against the acquisition of unwarranted influence, whether sought or unsought, by the military-industrial complex. The potential for the disastrous rise of misplaced power exists and will persist."

Dwight D. Eisenhower, Farewell Address, January 17, 1961

The World in 1961

Dwight D. Eisenhower's nickname was "Ike." He was a national hero before he became president. He led the Allies to victory over Nazi Germany in World War II, then served as the Supreme Allied Commander of Europe and the president of Columbia University before his two terms in the White House. Like another old general-turned-president, George Washington, Eisenhower used his farewell address to both say good-bye to public life and give Americans some advice.

The economy was booming, and the culture was changing. Americans were listening to new music, like Elvis. They were watching new television shows like *I Love Lucy* and *Leave It to Beaver*. There was a baby boom, as hundreds of thousands of World War II veterans returned home and started families, then moved to the growing suburbs outside of city centers. Eisenhower's administration had advanced civil rights, including the integration of public schools. Those fights for equality would continue in the 1960s.

Words Have a Purpose

Eisenhower was worried about what he called the "military-industrial complex," a combination of government power and corporate interests that, together, were gaining influence over American life and government spending. This was the Cold War, and Eisenhower recognized that the United States needed many ships, planes, tanks, and other military equipment to compete with the Soviet Union. Being a world power wasn't cheap, and the country was spending an enormous amount of money on the military; more than 9 percent of America's economic activity in 1961 went to defense. But if the real power in Washington was going to remain aligned with the country's values of freedom and democracy, *the American people* needed more of a say.

Words Make a Difference

The messenger can sometimes matter as much as the message—and Dwight D. Eisenhower was a great messenger to issue this warning. America trusted him on military matters because he was the most famous general alive. Many had served under General Eisenhower in World War II. If anyone knew how to run a military, and what it needed, it was Eisenhower.

Eisenhower's farewell address was the most famous one since George Washington's in 1796. In it, he talked about many issues, but the phrase "military-industrial complex" in particular has stuck in Americans' vocabularies. Thanks to Eisenhower's warning, many Americans remain watchful about the potential for "misplaced power" that can arise from the combination of military and business interests.

When he ran for president, Eisenhower had a catchy campaign slogan: "I like Ike!" He may have been a gruff, military man. But he could be charming. Because so many Americans liked Ike, he won in a landslide in both 1952 and 1956.

JOHN F. KENNEDY

"We choose to go to the moon in this decade and do the other things, not because they are easy, but because they are hard."

John F. Kennedy, Address at Rice University on the Nation's Space Effort, September 12, 1962

NEWS

The World in 1962

The United States and the Soviet Union were the two most powerful countries in the world. They were competing in every domain: economic, ideological, and military.

Technology was the new frontier for the Cold War, and the competition between the United States and the Soviet Union was now taking place in space. In October 1957, the Soviet Union launched Sputnik, the first satellite to orbit the Earth. Then, in 1961, Moscow sent the first person into space. While policymakers on Earth tried to keep the Cold War from turning hot, scientists were working to one-up each other in the Space Race. It looked like the Soviets might soon earn the biggest achievement of all: getting to the moon.

Words Have a Purpose

John F. Kennedy knew that the Soviet Union winning the Space Race would not only embarrass the United States; it would prove that America's biggest rival had the technological edge. So Kennedy decided to go for gold—or in this case, the moon.

Kennedy used his speech to rally the nation, setting a goal for the United States to "go to the moon in this decade" and show the world that America was leading the Space Race. He sought to inspire Americans by promising to achieve something that *no one* had ever done before.

But Kennedy needed Congress's help too. The research and technology necessary to get to the moon would require a *lot* of money. If Kennedy wanted the government to fund a mission to the moon, he first needed to ensure that the idea was popular with the American people—which is where speeches come in handy.

Words Make a Difference

Kennedy's speech worked! The American people and Congress got behind him, paying for the new National Aeronautics and Space Administration (NASA) and the Apollo program—one of the most expensive American scientific programs in history. The investment paid off. On July 20, 1969, the Apollo 11 shuttle landed on the moon, and Neil Armstrong became the first person to walk on its surface. As promised, Kennedy's dream had been achieved "in this decade."

America had accomplished something that no other country had achieved, and in doing so won the Space Race. And the success of the Apollo program inspired future generations of Americans to believe that anything is possible. Kennedy's determined message resonates even today, and modern leaders often describe their boldest plans as "moonshots."

☞ DID YOU KNOW?

John F. Kennedy was just forty-three years old when he took office, making him the youngest president ever elected (Theodore Roosevelt was forty-two when McKinley was assassinated). Many Americans were excited to turn on the television (a popular but still quite new medium) and see a young, handsome president with a glamorous wife and young kids in the White House. The Kennedy administration has since been called America's Camelot.

LYNDON B. JOHNSON

"What happened in Selma is part of a far larger movement which reaches into every section and State of America. It is the effort of [Black Americans] to secure for themselves the full blessings of American life. Their cause must be our cause too. Because it is not just [Black Americans], but really it is all of us, who must overcome the crippling legacy of bigotry and injustice. And we shall overcome."

Lyndon B. Johnson, Address to a Joint Session of Congress on Voting Legislation, March 15, 1965

The World in 1965

Vice President Lyndon B. Johnson became president when John F. Kennedy was assassinated on November 22, 1963, in Dallas, Texas. He then won reelection in his own right in 1964. Johnson's victory came on the heels of the Civil Rights Act of 1964, which outlawed discrimination based on race, sex, religion, or country of origin and ended state and local Jim Crow laws.

But a new law didn't mean the fight for justice and equality was over. America was reminded of this in 1965, when civil rights marchers—led by John Lewis and Reverend Hosea Williams—were brutally attacked by Alabama Highway Patrol troopers while marching across the Edmund Pettus Bridge in Selma, Alabama. The attack, a day that came to be known as "Bloody Sunday," shocked the country, who watched the violence unfold on their televisions. The images from Alabama horrified many, leading to the passage of the Voting Rights Act of 1965, another hard-won civil rights victory.

36

Words Have a Purpose

Before he was president, Lyndon B. Johnson wasn't an obvious champion of civil rights—far from it. As Senate Majority Leader, he'd watered down civil rights legislation so that it could pass a divided chamber, and he'd sometimes opposed other pieces of civil rights legislation.

But in the first few months of his presidency, Johnson's civil rights advocacy went beyond John F. Kennedy's work. Maybe it took someone like Johnson—who, unlike Kennedy, had the trust of Southern congressmen and many strong relationships in Congress—to help advance civil rights legislation in the 1960s. When Johnson told his audience that "[the civil rights activists'] cause must be our cause too," he was reminding Congress that it was *every* American's responsibility to take up the cause and work toward equal rights for all.

Words Make a Difference

The 1960s saw significant advances for the civil rights of Black Americans. Now, it was illegal for restaurants and diners to seat white Americans and Black Americans separately. Black Americans could no longer be forced to sit behind white Americans in the back of buses. And discriminatory voting laws, including literacy tests, were formally outlawed.

The majority of this change was due to the grassroots work of leaders like Martin Luther King Jr. and Rosa Parks. But without presidential support, and the support of many Americans who also believed that "their cause must be our cause too," Jim Crow laws would likely have remained on the books much longer. When Lyndon B. Johnson declared that the United States could overcome its "crippling legacy of bigotry and injustice," his words helped bend the arc of history toward justice.

If Lyndon B. Johnson didn't enter politics, he might have been a teacher. He'd graduated from Southwest Texas State Teachers College and taught in Texas high schools.

RICHARD NIXON

"Therefore, I shall resign the Presidency effective at noon tomorrow. Vice President Ford will be sworn in as President at that hour in this office."

Richard Nixon, Resignation Speech, August 8, 1974

The World in 1974

Today, when people think of Richard Nixon's presidency, they remember the scandal that ended it. Watergate only ended when Nixon resigned in disgrace. But Nixon's presidency wasn't just about scandal. During his time in office, the United States landed a man on the moon. In 1972, Nixon went to China and initiated America's engagement with the People's Republic. And in 1973, America withdrew its troops from Vietnam after a long war that resulted in millions of deaths—civilian and soldier alike.

Nixon had once been popular, winning election in 1968 and reelection in 1972 in two landslide victories. But his Republican campaign operatives had broken into the Democratic National Committee's office at the Watergate Hotel in Washington, DC. They'd installed listening devices to spy and help win the 1972 election. There were even members of the White House who knew about the break-in. But rather than coming clean, they covered it up. Then Nixon himself lied about it.

On August 8, 1974, Richard Nixon stepped down as commander in chief. He is the only American president to ever resign.

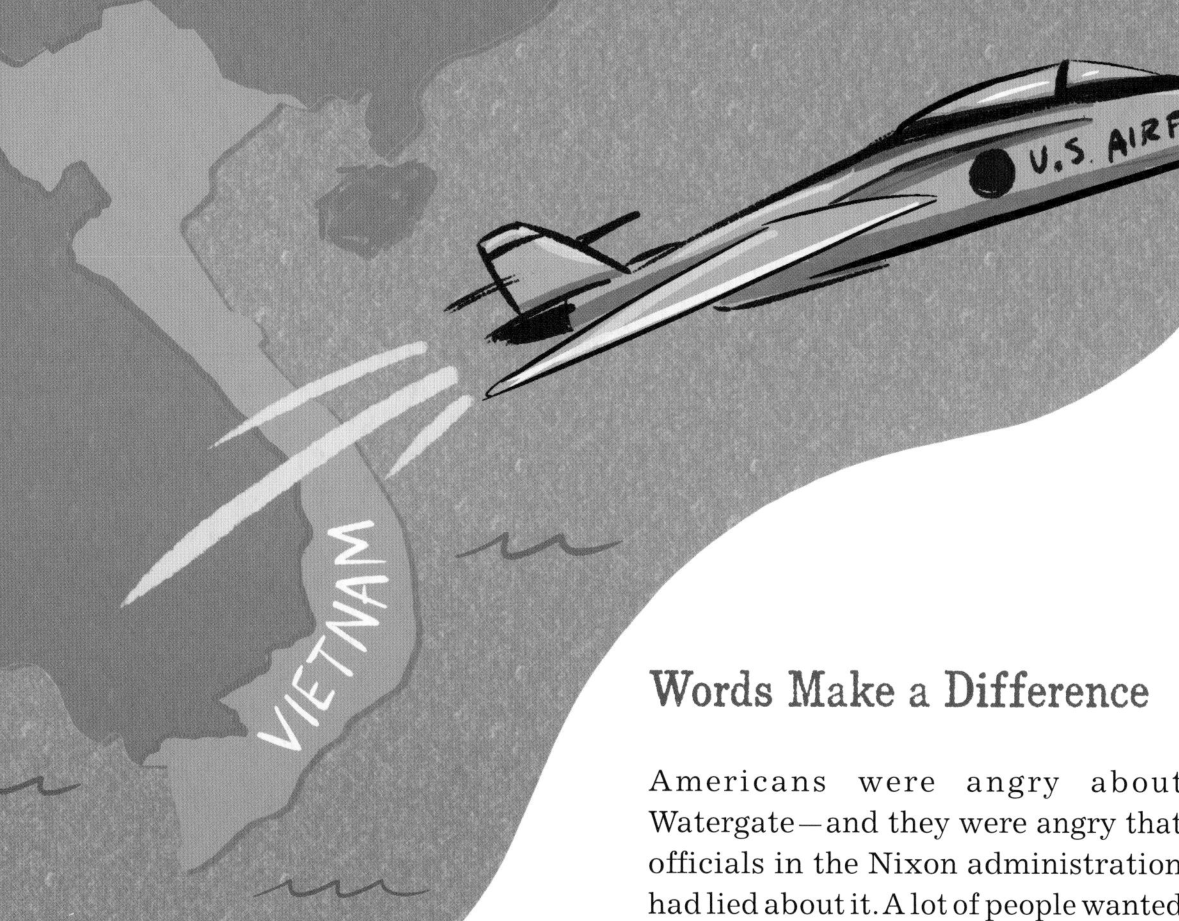

Words Have a Purpose

Richard Nixon said that announcing his resignation was "the most difficult sentence I shall ever have to speak." And it was. No president had ever resigned, and Nixon was disgraced. Because this event was unprecedented, no one knew what would happen next.

Nixon no longer had the trust of the American people. Gerald R. Ford had only been vice president for nine months, and Nixon had appointed him to the job. Now, Ford was about to become the president.

Words Make a Difference

Americans were angry about Watergate—and they were angry that officials in the Nixon administration had lied about it. A lot of people wanted to see Richard Nixon be impeached, or even jailed. Many Americans wondered whether they could truly trust *any* president ever again. From then on, whenever a major political scandal came to light, people have sometimes added the suffix "-gate" to the end of its name, as a nod to Watergate.

NIXON RESIGNS

Richard Nixon is the only person in American history to win the vice presidency twice (with Dwight D. Eisenhower in 1952 and 1956) *and* the presidency twice (in 1968 and 1972).

GERALD R. FORD

"My fellow Americans, our long national nightmare is over."

Gerald R. Ford, Remarks upon Taking the Oath of Office as President, August 9, 1974

The World in 1974

The last few years had been a nightmare. Richard Nixon had resigned in disgrace. The Vietnam War had cost many lives and ended without victory. The economy wasn't doing well; many people couldn't even find gas to fill up their cars, and there were gas lines that stretched around city blocks. To top it all off, Gerald R. Ford had not actually been elected president—he'd only gotten the job because his boss had resigned. Now, during his first address to the nation, the new president knew he needed to reassure Americans that this turmoil was finally over.

38

Words Have a Purpose

Many Americans lost faith in their government after Watergate. It seemed like elected officials were only looking out for themselves, and that the laws that applied to most Americans were not being followed by their leaders. Everyday citizens wanted reassurance that the government of the people still worked *for* the people. Ford's job was to reassure Americans. He needed to prove to them that *no one* is above the law.

Words Make a Difference

People trusted Gerald R. Ford. He had a reputation as an honest straight shooter. He wasn't well-known before the White House, but he was well-liked by those who did know him. And after Richard Nixon, honest Ford seemed like a refreshing change of pace. He was a steady hand in a moment when many Americans' trust in politicians had reached a low point.

As one of his first acts in office, Ford had to decide what to do about former President Nixon. A lot of Americans wanted Nixon to be held accountable for everything that had gone wrong during Watergate, and maybe even stand trial. But instead, Ford pardoned Nixon for any and all crimes he may have committed while in office. This move was not popular, and some members of the public saw this decision as a sign that Ford was no different from other politicians. They felt that maybe the national nightmare *wasn't* over.

☞ DID YOU KNOW?

Before he went into politics, Gerald R. Ford was a football star. During college, he played on the University of Michigan's national-championship-winning team, the Wolverines. He even received offers to play on two NFL teams: the Detroit Lions and the Green Bay Packers. But instead of going pro, he went to law school. What might have been?!

It was a tough call for Ford. But *not* pardoning Nixon would have had consequences too. Tensions were already high, and if Nixon were prosecuted, the national conversation could get even more divisive. Still, pardoning Nixon may have later cost Ford the 1976 election.

JIMMY CARTER

"It is a crisis that strikes at the very heart and soul and spirit of our national will. We can see this crisis in the growing doubt about the meaning of our own lives and in the loss of a unity of purpose for our Nation. The erosion of our confidence in the future is threatening to destroy the social and the political fabric of America."

Jimmy Carter, Address to the Nation on Energy and National Goals, July 15, 1979

The World in 1979

Americans were not happy. Unemployment was up, and so was inflation. There were still gas shortages across the country. And memories of Watergate were still fresh in the American people's minds.

The situation abroad looked even worse. The Cold War was still going on, and now it looked like the Soviet Union might win. It had secured more influence in Latin America and was looking to expand its power in many other countries, including Afghanistan, which it invaded in December. In Iran, the old king (known as the shah) fell during the Islamic Revolution—and just four months after Carter's speech, the revolutionaries took fifty-two Americans hostage for 444 days. Jimmy Carter knew that most Americans were skeptical about any of this improving anytime soon. They were very pessimistic.

Words Have a Purpose

Carter had a point: there *was* a crisis of confidence in America. In his televised address, he tried to diagnose the problem. He didn't think that the government could fix it. Carter said that Americans should both work harder and also cut down on the amount of stuff they were buying—in other words, "stop crying and start sweating."

Carter may have been right, but his prescription seemed off, and he was a poor messenger. His words didn't persuade many people that *he* was confident at all. Some listeners thought the president was suggesting that everything going wrong in the country was the American people's own fault. What many Americans took away from his speech wasn't a great call for unity or new policies—even though Carter did have a bunch of ideas! Instead, they heard the president telling them that things were bad (which they already knew) and Carter couldn't make them better.

Words Make a Difference

Words make a difference. But tone matters too. Carter didn't inspire confidence, and many Americans thought he sounded defeated. He spoke slowly, for thirty-three minutes, and when he talked about issues that could "destroy the social and political fabric of America," Americans didn't hear much to inspire them. Many people who watched the speech thought Carter was right about the crisis of confidence in America—but they'd also lost confidence in the American president.

DID YOU KNOW?

Jimmy Carter's speech is often called the "Malaise Speech." But that word never actually appeared in the text! The name stuck because "malaise" (meaning weakness, discomfort, and a sense of unease) is the impression Carter gave. Ronald Reagan tried to pick up on this when he ran against Carter in 1980. He declared, "I find no national malaise, I find nothing wrong with the American people."

RONALD REAGAN

"General Secretary Gorbachev, if you seek peace, if you seek prosperity for the Soviet Union and Eastern Europe, if you seek liberalization: Come here to this gate! Mr. Gorbachev, open this gate! Mr. Gorbachev, tear down this wall!"

Ronald Reagan, Remarks on East-West Relations at the Brandenburg Gate in West Berlin, June 12, 1987

The World in 1987

Germany was divided between east and west, and so was its capital, Berlin. Berlin had become the most potent symbol of the Cold War. The city was cut in two by a massive barrier called the Berlin Wall, which was built in 1961. On one side of the wall was democracy, and on the other was communism.

There had been ups and downs in the Reagan presidency, including the Iran-Contra scandal, where weapons were illegally sold to Iran and money was diverted to anti-communist forces in Nicaragua. But even Reagan's political rivals acknowledged that he was a great communicator and that the economy was improving. Reagan was serious about making a strong moral distinction between the United States and its democratic allies on the one hand, and the Soviet Union on the other. Meanwhile, the Soviet Union had a new leader, Mikhail Gorbachev, who seemed different from his predecessors. Gorbachev claimed he wanted to reform the Soviet system politically and economically. If he was serious, Reagan wanted him to prove it—and tear down the Berlin Wall.

Words Have a Purpose

To Ronald Reagan, the Cold War was about values: specifically, the values of democracy and freedom versus control and tyranny. And his speech was a challenge. Reagan wanted to test the new leader of the Soviet Union. Did Gorbachev mean what he was saying?

Reagan's speech was also a challenge to his audience of West Germans, as well as to those in East Germany who could hear his voice over the wall. They'd once lived side by side, but the Berlin Wall had been up for almost thirty years. Many Germans seemed used to it, even if they didn't like it. But Reagan urged his audience—on both sides of the wall—to imagine a world without it, something few even dared to hope for. That future could be theirs.

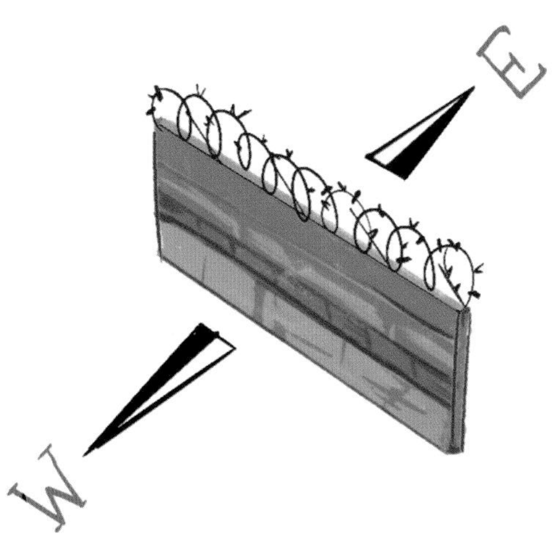

Words Make a Difference

After Reagan's speech, protests against the wall swept across East Germany. Then, on November 9, 1989, East Germans started heading for checkpoints to the West (the places where they could cross to the other side of the wall). For decades, the Soviet Union had kept people trapped and stopped all protests, sometimes with violence. But this time, they didn't.

The guards opened the gates, and East Germans began crossing to the West! There are tons of videos and pictures of Germans from both sides of Berlin climbing the wall, knocking it down with whatever tools they could find, and celebrating the country's reunification. You can check them out online.

☞ DID YOU KNOW?

The line "tear down this wall" may be the most famous line Reagan ever said. But it almost didn't make it into the speech! Many of Reagan's advisers didn't like it because they thought it was too provocative. They kept editing it out. But the president insisted on keeping it. And what the president says, goes.

GEORGE H. W. BUSH

"What is at stake is more than one small country; it is a big idea: a new world order, where diverse nations are drawn together in common cause to achieve the universal aspirations of mankind—peace and security, freedom, and the rule of law. Such is a world worthy of our struggle and worthy of our children's future."

George H. W. Bush, State of the Union Address, January 29, 1991

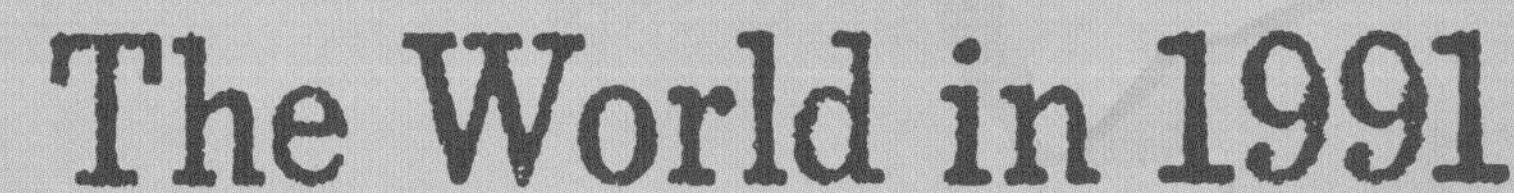

The World in 1991

The Cold War was almost over, and everyone knew it. By the close of 1991, Mikhail Gorbachev (the last leader of the Soviet Union) would resign. For almost five decades, the Cold War had defined so much of world politics. Few people could remember what life was like before the Soviet Union and the United States were competing across the globe. Now the world was left wondering: What's next?

The United States had recently turned its attention to the Middle East. Under the orders of its president and dictator Saddam Hussein, Iraq had invaded its smaller neighbor, Kuwait. In addition to this being a violation of international law, there were also concerns about the Iraqi tyrant controlling so much of the world's oil supply. George H. W. Bush believed that the United States' response was about more than one war—it was about the post–Cold War *world*.

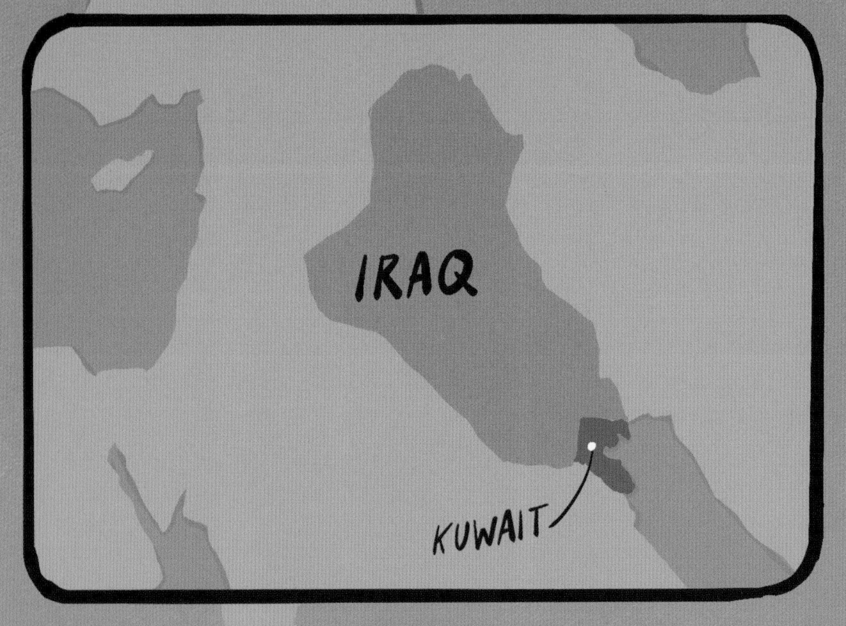

Words Have a Purpose

George H. W. Bush had a lot of experience in foreign policy. As a young man, he'd fought in World War II. He'd served in Congress, as the US ambassador to the United Nations and liaison to China, and as the director of the CIA during the Ford administration. And he'd been Ronald Reagan's vice president. George H. W. Bush was a critical player in America's victory in the Cold War.

In his State of the Union address, George H. W. Bush made the case that the war between Iraq and Kuwait wasn't about "one small country." It was about a future in which ideals of "peace and security, freedom, and the rule of law" would last. If this new post–Cold War world was going to be better than what came before, George H. W. Bush believed that the Iraqi dictator needed to be defeated, and that the United States needed to wield its moral authority as the most powerful country in the world to make sure that happened.

Words Make a Difference

When George H. W. Bush delivered his speech to Congress, American troops were already fighting in the Middle East, with the endorsement of the United Nations Security Council. They were on the battlefield alongside a coalition of dozens of countries from around the world—including Egypt, France, Saudi Arabia, the United Kingdom, and more. This conflict became known as the Gulf War.

The United States was the only global superpower left. With a victory against Iraq, George H. W. Bush hoped that the United States could chart a course to a future in which bigger countries didn't invade smaller countries; formerly communist countries would become liberal democracies; and the world would become a safer, freer, and more prosperous place for all.

DID YOU KNOW?

George H. W. Bush had an unusual birthday tradition. He loved skydiving—jumping out of a plane with a parachute! He did it on big birthdays, including when he turned ninety years old.

BILL CLINTON

"Our democracy must be not only the envy of the world but the engine of our own renewal. There is nothing wrong with America that cannot be cured by what is right with America."

Bill Clinton, First Inaugural Address, January 20, 1993

The World in 1993

The twentieth century was almost over. The Berlin Wall had fallen. The Cold War was over—and it had ended peacefully. At the same time, new technologies were emerging, and daily life was changing quickly. Among many other inventions, the early internet was capturing the public's imagination. More and more Americans were getting online.

America also had its first baby boomer president, Bill Clinton. Born in 1946 after World War II, Clinton was the second-youngest president ever elected, after John F. Kennedy. The old guard had passed the baton, and a new generation was in charge. Now those new leaders had to decide what was next for America.

Words Have a Purpose

Much was going right in the United States, but people knew that this trend might not last forever. In particular, many Americans were worried about the economy. In his inaugural address, Bill Clinton promised Americans that whatever problems the country faced, it could also find a way to solve them.

In the post–Cold War world, Clinton wanted the United States to be a model for other democracies. He also wanted Americans to have confidence that the United States *could* solve whatever social or economic challenges came its way. The people needed to focus on what was going *right* with America—and the country needed to invest in its people, new industries, and the future. This was an optimistic, hopeful message for the new president to deliver on his first day in office.

Words Make a Difference

Most Americans who think of the 1990s remember them fondly. The economy improved. There were plenty of new jobs in new industries. And new technologies promised a better future.

Things were working, even in Washington! For the first time in decades, the United States government ran a budget surplus (meaning that it spent less money than it took in). The country still faced major problems, like poverty and inequality, but there weren't major wars, and it seemed like Bill Clinton might be right: America had the power to fix whatever ailed it and lead the world by its example.

Bill Clinton, George W. Bush, and Donald Trump were all born in 1946, within a few months of one another. It was a very presidential year!

GEORGE W. BUSH

"I can hear you. I can hear you. The rest of the world hears you. And the people who knocked these buildings down will hear all of us soon."

George W. Bush, speaking at Ground Zero in New York City, September 14, 2001

The World in 2001

George W. Bush did not expect to be a wartime president. But on September 11, 2001, nineteen terrorists from the militant group al-Qaeda hijacked four commercial airplanes with hundreds of civilian passengers onboard. The terrorists flew two planes into the Twin Towers of the World Trade Center complex in New York City and one into the Pentagon (where the Department of Defense is headquartered) in Washington, DC. A fourth plane, likely headed toward the Capitol in Washington, DC, crashed onto an empty field in Shanksville, Pennsylvania, after the brave passengers fought back and seized control from the terrorists. In total, the terrorists killed nearly three thousand people that day—from both the United States and at least ninety other countries. The world would never be the same. America was at war.

43

☞ DID YOU KNOW?

George W. Bush took up painting after he left office. Among the people he painted were sixty-six veterans who fought in the Global War on Terrorism in Iraq and Afghanistan after September 11. He shared their stories in a book called *Portraits of Courage.*

Words Have a Purpose

Bush's remarks, delivered three days after the attacks, weren't scripted. There was no speechwriter helping the president. But they're some of the best-remembered of George W. Bush's presidency. The setting (Ground Zero), the timing (9/14), the audience (New York City firefighters and police officers, who were still clearing the debris), and the message all came together in a moment that no one could have predicted.

At first, Bush began his speech by speaking into a bullhorn, but it wasn't loud enough. One person in the crowd yelled out, "I can't hear you!" Bush's spontaneous response to that anonymous audience member ("*I* can hear *you!*") united the crowd and the country, letting them know that the world was with New York and America in their grief and determination. There were massive cheers. It was clear that the United States wouldn't let the act of terrorism go unanswered.

Words Make a Difference

The horrors of September 11 were still fresh on Americans' minds. Many Americans couldn't believe what had happened. The United States had not been attacked at home on such a scale since Pearl Harbor.

Now, just three days after the attack, they saw their president standing on top of a pile of rubble that had once been the tallest buildings in New York City. Bush's arm was around a New York City firefighter who was performing search and rescue operations. Americans were heartbroken and scared. They wanted to know how the United States would respond—and Bush's words that day were a promise that America would take the fight to al-Qaeda.

BARACK OBAMA

"*Yes, we can.*"

Barack Obama, New Hampshire Democratic Primary Speech, January 8, 2008

The World in 2008

It was an election year, and both the Republican and Democratic parties had to decide who their nominees would be. This was an uncertain time—and with the economy heading toward a recession, Americans were worried. Wars in Afghanistan and Iraq were still going on, and they didn't look like they were going to end anytime soon. Many Americans didn't approve of how the wars were handled, and they blamed both the government and big businesses for the struggling economy.

These factors made room for a relative political newcomer, Barack Obama, to become one of the leading contenders for the White House. In 2008, Obama promised "hope and change" for the American people, and that's exactly what many wanted. Obama was running against Hillary Clinton, a former senator and first lady. But after Obama's victory in the Iowa caucuses (the first nominating event), it was clear that this rising political star might be able to do more than compete for the Democratic nomination—he might win the election in November! The candidate who confidently promised America "yes, we can" was about to show just how much *he* could accomplish.

Words Have a Purpose

Barack Obama's candidacy gave many Americans hope. Obama promised big changes during his presidency, proposing new ideas for America's economy, domestic policy, and foreign affairs. With his speeches, he wanted voters to believe that they could be a part of making that change.

This message of optimism—that the country and its people could still accomplish great things—resonated with voters. Obama went on to win a historic victory in the November election, with his administration promising to shake up national politics in positive ways.

Words Make a Difference

"Yes, we can" was Barack Obama's motto. It featured in his campaign ads, and he said it not just at every campaign stop, but all throughout his presidency. Obama would become the first Black president in American history, and he entered office with a high approval rating.

Obama was a bold president with a bold agenda. He fought for health-care reform, marriage equality, and programs to boost economic recovery, as well as pushing for a major shift in US foreign policy all around the world. At the end of his presidency, after two terms in office, Obama delivered his farewell address in Chicago in January 2017. He ended his time in the White House by reflecting on his administration's accomplishments and returning once more to his favorite phrase, saying: "Yes, we did. Yes, we can."

Barack Obama and his future wife, Michelle Obama, met when Michelle was assigned to be Barack's mentor at work. Both graduates of Harvard Law School, the two were colleagues at a law firm in 1989. Twenty years later, now married and with two young daughters named Sasha and Malia, they were headed to the White House.

DONALD TRUMP

"*Make America great again.*"

Donald Trump, Presidential Campaign
Announcement Speech, June 16, 2015

The World in 2015

Donald Trump had just declared that he was running for president. And it was clear that the 2016 election would be unlike any before it. The economy had been growing for eight years straight, coming a long way from 2008's Great Recession. But the recovery was slow, and many people felt left behind. Wages still hadn't fully recovered. Few Americans were satisfied with the Bush and Obama administrations' attempts to reform the US immigration system. And the United States' global competitors, including China, appeared stronger than ever.

With Barack Obama's two-term presidency ending, the White House was up for grabs by either party. Who would be the next president? The Democrats rallied around Hillary Clinton, Obama's first secretary of state and a former senator and first lady. The Republicans were much less united. From their huge field of candidates, they ultimately nominated Donald Trump—a New York businessman who had never held an elected office before.

Words Have a Purpose

Words can mean different things to different people. To many of Donald Trump's supporters, "Make America Great Again" hearkened back to better days and looked forward to a more prosperous future. It reminded them of times in America's past when they thought the country had more economic, military, and political power. They hoped Trump would end the feeling of decline and bring the good times back.

To many people who opposed Trump, though, the phrase "Make America Great Again" was more threatening. In the context of other inflammatory campaign rhetoric, the slogan reminded them of times in the past when many Americans were denied their civil rights, facing discrimination and violence. They remembered some of the darkest chapters in United States history and feared that Trump was pledging to roll back protections and enact new policies that would make life worse for America's most vulnerable citizens—including racial and religious minorities, disabled people, immigrants, and women.

Words Make a Difference

Donald Trump was an unlikely president of the United States. Usually, there are two ways to get elected president. Either you served in an elected office (as a governor, a senator, or the vice president), or you were a general who won a war (like Ulysses S. Grant or Dwight D. Eisenhower). Trump did neither. He'd never been a politician before, and he had never served in the military—he was a businessman and a TV celebrity from a wealthy family. But although Hillary Clinton won the popular vote by 2.8 million votes, Trump's wild campaign, wide media coverage, and celebrity status managed to put him over the top in the Electoral College. The Trump campaign had been unlike any before it. And his presidency would be too.

DID YOU KNOW?

Before Donald Trump was president, he hosted a reality TV show. It was called *The Apprentice*, and different contestants competed to show off their business skills. Some of the people who served in Trump's administration were previously contestants on *The Apprentice*.

JOE BIDEN

"We must end this uncivil war that pits red against blue, rural versus urban, conservative versus liberal."

Joe Biden, Inaugural Address, January 20, 2021

The World in 2021

Joe Biden's inauguration took place at an extraordinary—and extraordinarily challenging—moment in American history. The COVID-19 pandemic was entering its second year and vaccines were finally becoming available. But hundreds of thousands of Americans had died from the disease, and millions more had gotten sick. The recovering economy had been in free fall. And tensions abroad, particularly with China and Russia, were rising.

But on Inauguration Day, all of this paled in comparison to what had happened two weeks prior. On January 6, 2021, a violent group of Trump supporters stormed the United States Capitol—the site of the inauguration where Biden was now speaking. The mob had forced its way inside and tried to disrupt the vote counting—perhaps even hoping to overturn the election results—while threatening violence against lawmakers.

The country was shaken. The United States' peaceful transfer of power—a hallmark of American democracy since the days of George Washington—was no longer taken for granted. The stakes were high on Inauguration Day, as Americans looked to the Capitol and wondered what Joe Biden would say.

46

Words Have a Purpose

Even before the storming of the Capitol, the country was bitterly divided. Democrats and Republicans distrusted one another. And Donald Trump, who had encouraged the mob, didn't attend his successor's inauguration—the first time this had happened in more than a hundred years.

Joe Biden had received more popular votes than any candidate in history (over eighty million!). In his inaugural address, the new president acknowledged America's very real divisions and spoke about the importance of overcoming them, urging *all* Americans—Republican and Democrat, rural and urban, of all races and creeds—to come together for the good of the country. The theme of the speech was "unity"; Biden said that word eight times in his inaugural address.

Words Make a Difference

Presidents can use their speeches, especially big ones like inaugural addresses, to take stock of current events and reassure the country. And after a year of chaos, sickness, loss, and unprecedented challenges to democracy, America was looking for reassurance. Joe Biden's words were meant to promise the American people that the temperature of the country was going to cool down and that the United States *could* be united again.

Inauguration Day went off without a hitch—despite taking place during a global pandemic, just two weeks after a mob assaulted the Capitol. Witnessing this familiar democratic tradition gave many Americans a big boost of confidence. Now, what remained to be seen was whether the new president could actually keep his promises. After all, uniting a country in practice is much tougher than delivering one speech.

DID YOU KNOW?

Joe Biden was seventy-eight years old when he took office, making him the oldest American president ever elected. He was first elected to the Senate in 1972, during the Nixon administration—and right around Watergate!

PRESIDENTIAL

1789

★ GEORGE WASHINGTON ★
(TWO TERMS, 1789–1797)

George Washington is inaugurated as the first president of the United States.

1791

The Bill of Rights is ratified.

1796

Washington delivers his farewell address, establishing the two-term precedent.

1797

★ JOHN ADAMS ★
(ONE TERM, 1797–1801)

1800

The US capital is moved from Philadelphia to Washington, DC.

1817

★ JAMES MONROE ★
(TWO TERMS, 1817–1825)

1820

The Missouri Compromise is passed.

1823

The Monroe Doctrine is declared.

1825

★ JOHN QUINCY ADAMS ★
(ONE TERM, 1825–1829)

1829

★ ANDREW JACKSON ★
(TWO TERMS, 1829–1837)

1849

★ ZACHARY TAYLOR ★
(ONE TERM, 1849–1850)

1850

Taylor dies in office and is succeeded by Vice President Millard Fillmore.

★ MILLARD FILLMORE ★
(ONE TERM, 1850–1853)

The Compromise of 1850 is passed.

1853

★ FRANKLIN PIERCE ★
(ONE TERM, 1853–1857)

1854

The Kansas-Nebraska Act is passed, leading to violence in the two new territories.

1857

★ JAMES BUCHANAN ★
(ONE TERM, 1857–1861)

1869

★ ULYSSES S. GRANT ★
(TWO TERMS, 1869–1877)

The Fifteenth Amendment to the Constitution is passed.

1877

★ RUTHERFORD B. HAYES ★
(ONE TERM, 1877–1881)

The Compromise of 1877 ends Reconstruction in the South.

1881

★ JAMES A. GARFIELD ★
(ONE TERM, 1881)

Garfield is assassinated and succeeded by Vice President Chester A. Arthur.

★ CHESTER A. ARTHUR ★
(ONE TERM, 1881–1885)

1883

The Pendleton Civil Service Act establishes a merit-based system for federal jobs.

1885

★ GROVER CLEVELAND ★
(FIRST OF TWO TERMS, 1885–1889)

TIME LINE

1801

★ THOMAS JEFFERSON ★
(TWO TERMS, 1801–1809)

1803

The Louisiana Purchase from France doubles the size of the United States.

1804–1806

The Lewis and Clark Expedition maps territory acquired in the Louisiana Purchase.

1809

★ JAMES MADISON ★
(TWO TERMS, 1809–1817)

1812–1815

The War of 1812 is fought between the United States and Great Britain.

1830

The Indian Removal Act leads to the forced relocation of Native American tribes and the Trail of Tears.

1837

★ MARTIN VAN BUREN ★
(One term, 1837–1841)

1841

★ WILLIAM HENRY HARRISON ★
(ONE TERM, 1841)

Harrison dies after only one month in office and is succeeded by Vice President John Tyler.

★ JOHN TYLER ★
(ONE TERM, 1841–1845)

1845

JAMES K. POLK ★
(ONE TERM, 1845–1849)

The United States annexes Texas.

1846–1848

The US and Mexico fight the Mexican-American War.

1860

Southern states begin to secede.

1861

★ ABRAHAM LINCOLN ★
(TWO TERMS, 1861–1865)

The Civil War begins with the Confederate attack on Fort Sumter.

1863

Lincoln issues the Emancipation Proclamation.

The Union defeats the Confederacy at the Battle of Gettysburg.

1865

Confederate General Robert E. Lee surrenders to General Ulysses S. Grant.

Lincoln is assassinated and is succeeded by Vice President Andrew Johnson.

★ ANDREW JOHNSON ★ (ONE TERM, 1865–1869)

The Thirteenth and Fourteenth Amendments to the Constitution are passed.

1868

Johnson becomes the first president to be impeached by the House of Representatives. He is acquitted by the Senate by a single vote.

1889

★ BENJAMIN HARRISON ★
(ONE TERM, 1889–1893)

1893

★ GROVER CLEVELAND ★
(SECOND OF TWO TERMS, 1893–1897)

1897

★ WILLIAM MCKINLEY ★
(TWO TERMS, 1897–1901)

1898

The US wins the Spanish-American War and acquires the territories of Puerto Rico, Guam, and the Philippines.

1901

McKinley is assassinated and succeeded by Vice President Theodore Roosevelt.

★ THEODORE ROOSEVELT ★
(TWO TERMS, 1901–1909)

PRESIDENTIAL

1909

★ **WILLIAM HOWARD TAFT** ★
(ONE TERM, 1909–1913)

1913

★ **WOODROW WILSON** ★
(TWO TERMS, 1913–1921)

1917

The United States enters World War I.

1919

The Treaty of Versailles is signed, ending World War I and establishing the League of Nations.

1920

The Nineteenth Amendment is ratified, giving women the right to vote.

1941

The United States enters World War II after the Japanese attack on Pearl Harbor.

1945

★ **HARRY S. TRUMAN** ★
(TWO TERMS, 1945–1953)

Truman makes the decision to drop atomic bombs on Hiroshima and Nagasaki, leading to Japan's surrender in World War II.

1947

The Truman Doctrine is announced near the start of the Cold War.

1953

★ **DWIGHT D. EISENHOWER** ★
(TWO TERMS, 1953–1961)

1954

The Supreme Court case *Brown v. Board of Education* declares segregation in public schools unconstitutional.

1968

The Vietnam War escalates with the Tet Offensive.

1969

★ **RICHARD NIXON** ★
(TWO TERMS, 1969–1974)

The Apollo 11 mission successfully lands the first humans on the moon.

1972

President Nixon travels to China and establishes US engagement with the People's Republic of China.

1974

President Nixon resigns after the Watergate scandal.

★ **GERALD R. FORD** ★
(ONE TERM, 1974–1977)

1975

The Vietnam War ends with the fall of Saigon.

1991

The collapse of the Soviet Union marks the end of the Cold War.

1993

★ **BILL CLINTON** ★
(TWO TERMS, 1993–2001)

1998

Clinton is impeached by the House of Representatives but acquitted by the Senate.

2001

★ **GEORGE W. BUSH** ★
(TWO TERMS, 2001–2009)

The September 11 attacks lead to the invasion of Afghanistan and the war on terrorism.

2009

★ **BARACK OBAMA** ★
(TWO TERMS, 2009–2017)

TIME LINE

1921

★ WARREN G. HARDING ★
(ONE TERM, 1921–1923)

1923

Harding dies in office and is succeeded by Vice President Calvin Coolidge.

★ CALVIN COOLIDGE ★
(TWO TERMS, 1923–1929)

1929

★ HERBERT HOOVER ★
(ONE TERM, 1929–1933)

The Great Depression begins.

1933

★ FRANKLIN D. ROOSEVELT ★
(FOUR TERMS, 1933–1945)

1933–1939

The New Deal is passed in an attempt to end the Great Depression.

1961

★ JOHN F. KENNEDY ★
(ONE TERM, 1961–1963)

1962

The Cuban Missile Crisis brings the United States and the Soviet Union to the brink of nuclear war.

1963

Kennedy is assassinated and is succeeded by Vice President Lyndon B. Johnson.

★ LYNDON B. JOHNSON ★
(TWO TERMS, 1963–1969)

1964

The Civil Rights Act of 1964 prohibits discrimination based on race, color, religion, sex, or national origin.

1965

The Voting Rights Act of 1965 is signed into law.

1977

★ JIMMY CARTER ★
(ONE TERM, 1977–1981)

1979–1981

The Iran hostage crisis lasts for 444 days.

1981

★ RONALD REAGAN ★
(TWO TERMS, 1981–1989)

1989

★ GEORGE H. W. BUSH ★
(ONE TERM, 1989–1993)

1990

The Gulf War begins with a US-led coalition driving Iraqi forces out of Kuwait.

2015

The Supreme Court case *Obergefell v. Hodges* declares the constitutional right of gay and lesbian couples to marry.

2017

★ DONALD TRUMP ★
(ONE TERM, 2017–2021)

2019–2020

Trump is impeached by the House of Representatives but acquitted by the Senate.

2020

COVID-19 is declared a global pandemic.

2021

A pro-Trump mob storms the US Capitol in an unsuccessful attempt to change the outcome of the 2020 election, leading to Trump's second impeachment.

★ JOE BIDEN ★
(ONE TERM, 2021–PRESENT)

DELIVERING YOUR MESSAGE

Tips for Aspiring Speechwriters (and Aspiring Presidents)

Human beings have been working on the art of speechwriting and speechmaking for as long as they've been writing and talking. It was in the fourth century BC that Aristotle first laid out the concepts of ethos (appeals to the character of the audience), pathos (appeals to the audience's emotions and sensibilities), and logos (appeals to the audience's logic) to describe how a speaker can persuade an audience.

It's been nearly 2,500 years since then, and there's still no formula for what to write or say to get your message across perfectly—even if artificial intelligence tools like ChatGPT are doing their best to figure it out. Writing essays, letters, or speeches isn't easy. And delivering them out loud can be even harder! But these are effective ways to make your arguments and to ensure that what you write and say really does make a difference. Your words matter. And you too can shape history—just like the presidents in this book!

Here are ten tips to keep in mind as you begin your persuasive writing journey:

1 - Know what you want to say. This may seem obvious, but in fact, not everyone does! Sometimes, even after a twenty-minute speech, a speaker's audience is left asking, "What was all *that* about?"

2 - Know your audience. Take some time to understand the group you're speaking to and the occasion for which they're assembled. Is it a school assembly? An annual meeting? A public hearing? What was said the last time this group got together, and what's on their minds today? Research will improve your speech, and it's a sign of respect for your audience—who will be more likely to hear you out because of it.

3 - Every good speech has a structure. This can be a theme, a story, a metaphor, or something else. There's an old adage for one way to help give structure to a speech: "Tell 'em what you're going to tell 'em; then tell 'em; then tell 'em what you told 'em."

4 - A speech is meant to be spoken. As you're writing, try saying the words out loud. If it's hard for you to say, it will also be hard for your audience to hear or understand.

5 - On that note: a speaker needs to be able to breathe. Long sentences can be fun to write. But they're difficult to say! Feel free to use em dashes, commas, periods, and all manner of punctuation marks to give yourself a moment of relief between the words.

6 - Don't use words that are hard to say. You'll stumble. William Safire, President Nixon's speechwriter, had some good counsel on this front: "[B]eware of undeliverable words. 'Undeliverable' is one such trip word." Here's some more advice from Safire: "Avoid clichés like the plague."

7 - Most of your speech will be forgotten. A speech may last for fifteen minutes, but a week later people will only remember about fifteen seconds. So make those fifteen seconds count! We all know the line, "the only thing we have to fear is fear itself." But how many people can recall the rest of FDR's first inaugural address? Especially in an era of social media, tweets, sound bites, and quotable lines will help your message last.

8 - Editors are your friends. When you finish your first, second, or third drafts, send them to people you trust. Ask them for honest feedback. They'll tell you what you're getting right—and more importantly, what you *aren't* getting right yet.

9 - More on that last point: don't take edits personally. A line may sound brilliant to you, but it might not make sense to anyone else. When this happens, take out a red pen or hit the backspace. After all, if you want your message to be heard, it's most important that people understand what you're saying! When you have to make a tough edit, remember the alleged words of William Faulkner, who said, "In writing, you must kill all your darlings."

10 - Finish what you started. To end on a high note and stick in people's minds, every speech needs to bring its audience in for an exciting landing, be it with a rallying cry or a reminder of the importance of the occasion. Your conclusion is your last chance to get your message across—so use it!

WHAT IF?

Speeches the Presidents Never Gave

There's a big question hanging over history: *What if?*

Historical events didn't have to unfold the way they did. When the Founding Fathers signed their names to the Declaration of Independence, they didn't know whether they'd win the Revolutionary War. *What if they lost?* They'd likely have been executed by King George III. This possibility was certainly on everyone's minds at the time.

Asking the question *What if?* means thinking about history in a whole new way. Historians study the past to figure out what happened and why. But they also consider all the things that might have happened instead. *What if there hadn't been a Revolutionary War at all? What if the Union had lost the Civil War? What if the Great Depression had never happened? What if . . . ?* The questions go on and on.

Of course, everyone asks these kinds of questions, not just historians! Think about some of your own *What if*'s. *What if I had tried harder on that test? What if I had been nicer to that person? What if I had a superpower?* Your questions can probably go on and on too!

Decision-makers, such as the president, also ask *What if?* every day. Before acting, they look at options, weigh the pros and cons, and decide what to do based on the best information they have at that moment. But the entire process starts with asking the question: *What if?* After all, every action has consequences, and every word has the potential to shape history.

In this last section of this book, we'll look at three speeches that the president—or in Eisenhower's case, future president—was prepared to give, but never did. These speeches could also have changed history. But then other events unfolded, and they were never given. Each speech is an invitation for us to think about the big questions in our own lives, such as how we got to where we are, where we want to go, and how we want to get there.

Right now, though, you've got a more timely question ahead of you: *What if you finish this book?* You're almost there! And what comes after that will be up to *you*.

What If the D-Day Invasion Failed?

General Dwight D. Eisenhower, "In Case of Failure"

June 5, 1944

On the night of June 5, 1944, General Dwight D. Eisenhower didn't get much sleep. He was the Supreme Allied Commander, and June 6 was D-Day (a military term for the day on which a combat operation is scheduled to take place). The Allies—including the United States, the United Kingdom, Canada, and France—were about to invade France, which had fallen under the control of Nazi Germany, and attempt to liberate Western Europe from the Nazi regime. This would be one of the most ambitious and difficult operations in recorded history. Hundreds of thousands of people were involved—on land, in the air, and at sea. If they were successful, the Allies would win World War II. But if they failed, the war might turn out very differently.

General Eisenhower visited his troops the night before D-Day, with only a few hours left before the invasion. He wanted to meet with the young men—many of them teenagers—who were fighting under his command. They were being asked to do what many thought would be impossible. Whatever happened next, General Eisenhower knew that he was responsible for the outcome of the D-Day invasion. He prayed for victory. But he was prepared for defeat.

Today, we know what happened: the Allies won and successfully liberated Europe. But what if they hadn't? What if the D-Day invasion had failed? How would World War II, and the rest of the twentieth century, have been different?

"Our landings in the Cherbourg-Havre area have failed to gain a satisfactory foothold and I have withdrawn the troops. My decision to attack at this time and place was based upon the best information available. The troops, the air and the Navy did all that bravery and devotion to duty could do. If any blame or fault attaches to the attempt it is mine alone."

What If John F. Kennedy Had Not Been Assassinated?

President John F. Kennedy, Remarks Prepared for Delivery at the Trade Mart in Dallas, Texas

November 22, 1963

It was November 22, 1963, and President John F. Kennedy was in a motorcade on his way to give a speech at the Trade Mart in Dallas, Texas. He was riding along a ten-mile tour of the city in an open-top 1961 Lincoln Continental four-door convertible. The car was going slowly (at an average of around eleven miles an hour) so that the President and Mrs. Kennedy could wave to the eager crowd that lined the street.

But President Kennedy never gave his speech, because he never made it to the Trade Mart. Just after noon, as the president's car was leaving Main Street at Dealey Plaza, a gunman opened fire. He hit the president and the governor of Texas, who was seated in the same convertible. The Secret Service rushed the president to a nearby hospital, but it was too late. John F. Kennedy was pronounced dead at around 1:00 p.m. Shortly after, police arrested the gunman, and President Kennedy was laid to rest at Arlington National Cemetery.

The speech that President Kennedy was prepared to give on the day of his assassination is a reminder of many of the themes of his presidency: America's high ideals, freedom, and strength. Those were the themes he was planning to run on in his reelection campaign in 1964. If he hadn't been assassinated, how could American history have turned out differently? How would we remember the legacy of John F. Kennedy today?

"We in this country, in this generation, are—by destiny rather than choice—the watchmen on the walls of world freedom. We ask, therefore, that we may be worthy of our power and responsibility, that we may exercise our strength with wisdom and restraint, and that we may achieve in our time and for all time the ancient vision of 'peace on earth, good will toward men.' That must always be our goal, and the righteousness of our cause must always underlie our strength. For as was written long ago: 'except the Lord keep the city, the watchman waketh but in vain.'"

What If the Moon Landing Had Failed?

President Richard Nixon, "In Event of Moon Disaster"

July 20, 1969

When astronaut Neil Armstrong set foot on the moon, he said some of the most famous words in history: "One small step for a man, one giant leap for mankind." But there was no guarantee that he would make it to the moon to take that small step. And even if he did, there was no guarantee that he'd make it back to Earth afterward. The president would need to have something to say to the grieving American people, and the world, if that happened.

This was a dangerous mission. Before July 20, 1969, no human being had ever set foot on the lunar surface. If all went as planned, commander Neil Armstrong and lunar module pilot Edwin "Buzz" Aldrin would make history as the first and second. It took Apollo 11 around 109 hours and forty-two minutes to make it to the moon. The entire time, President Nixon—and the country—hoped and prayed for the best. But the president also wondered: What if the mission failed? What if Armstrong and Aldrin never made it back from their mission to the moon?

The president prepared for that terrible outcome. He and his speechwriters drafted a set of remarks in case Neil Armstrong and Buzz Aldrin were stranded on the moon. It was a critical task—the world was watching, and people would need to hear from the president if the worst came to pass. More than five decades later, we know that the Apollo 11 mission succeeded. But President Nixon's planned remarks in the event of a moon disaster are a reminder of how daring the Apollo 11 mission really was—and how astronomically high the stakes of the Space Race were too.

"Fate has ordained that the men who went to the moon to explore in peace will stay on the moon to rest in peace.

These brave men, Neil Armstrong and Edwin Aldrin, know that there is no hope for their recovery. But they also know that there is hope for mankind in their sacrifice.

These two men are laying down their lives in mankind's most noble goal: the search for truth and understanding.

They will be mourned by their families and friends; they will be mourned by their nation; they will be mourned by the people of the world; they will be mourned by a Mother Earth that dared send two of her sons into the unknown.

In their exploration, they stirred the people of the world to feel as one; in their sacrifice, they bind more tightly the brotherhood of man.

In ancient days, men looked at stars and saw their heroes in the constellations. In modern times, we do much the same, but our heroes are epic men of flesh and blood.

Others will follow, and surely find their way home. Man's search will not be denied. But these men were the first, and they will remain the foremost in our hearts.

For every human being who looks up at the moon in the nights to come will know that there is some corner of another world that is forever mankind."